THE  ANIMAL WORLD

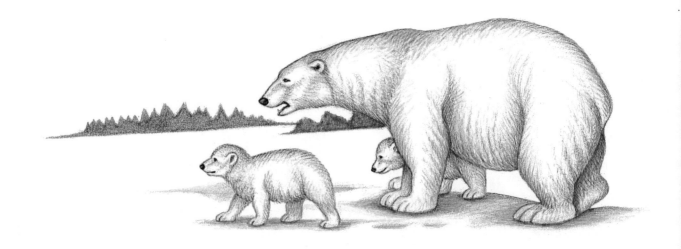

THE ANIMAL WORLD

BY Donald M. Silver, PH.D.

ILLUSTRATED BY

Patricia J. Wynne

Random House New York

For Lorraine Kirsch Silver, who found good in everything.

I would like to thank Janet Finnie, Melinda Luke, and Jos. Trautwein for their assistance and advice in editing and designing this book. Thanks also to Dr. Guy Musser of the American Museum of Natural History for his views on the animal world.

I am indebted to Andrew M. Wynne and Edward T. Riley for the inspiration they provided.

Donald M. Silver, Ph.D.

Key of Abbreviations
mm = millimeter (25.4 mm = 1 inch)
cm = centimeter (2.54 cm = 1 inch)
m = meter (0.3 m = 1 foot)
km = kilometer (1.6 km = 1 mile)
kph = kilometers per hour
kg = kilogram (0.45 kg = 1 pound)
0 degree Celsius (°C.) = 32° Fahrenheit (°F.)

BOOK DESIGN:
Bentwood Studio/Jos. Trautwein

Library of Congress Cataloging-in-Publication Data

Silver, Donald M.
    The animal world.
    (The Random House library of knowledge ; 8)
    Includes index.
    1. Zoology — Juvenile literature. I. Wynne, Patricia.
II. Title. III. Series.
QL48.2.S55 1987 591 86-3894
ISBN: 0-394-86650-9 (trade); 0-394-96650-3 (lib. bdg.)

Manufactured in the United States of America
1 2 3 4 5 6 7 8 9 0

CONTENTS

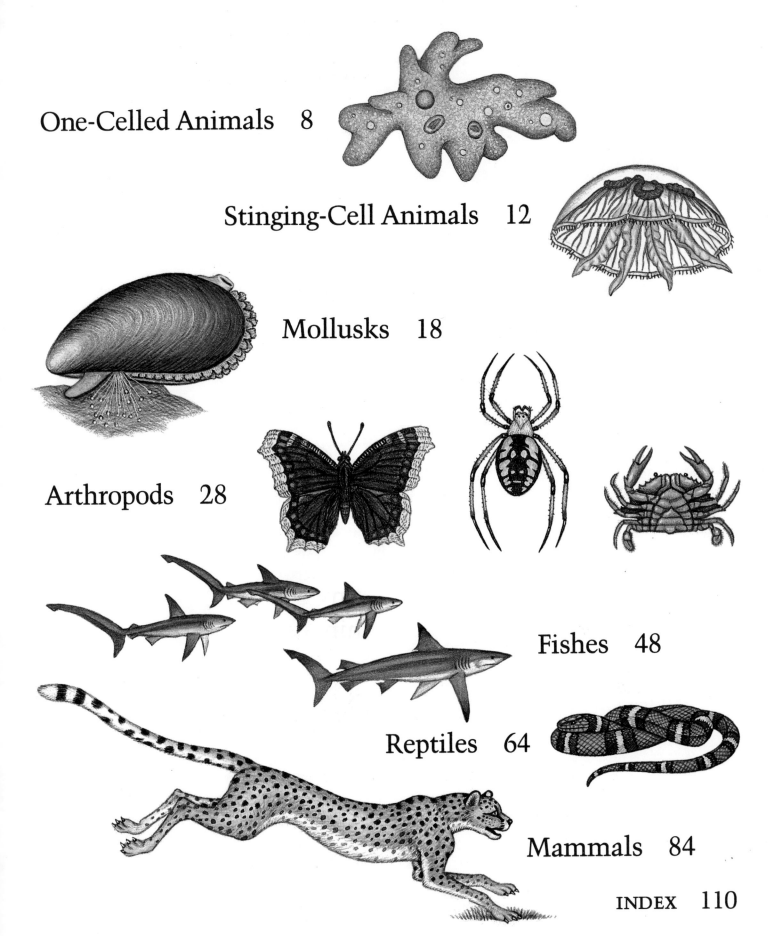

The Animal World

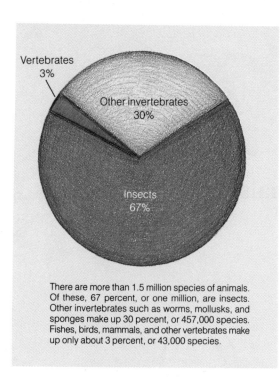

Vertebrates
3%

Other invertebrates
30%

Insects
67%

There are more than 1.5 million species of animals. Of these, 67 percent, or one million, are insects. Other invertebrates such as worms, mollusks, and sponges make up 30 percent, or 457,000 species. Fishes, birds, mammals, and other vertebrates make up only about 3 percent, or 43,000 species.

The animal world is all around us. Birds soar across the sky, spiders build their webs, and squirrels scurry up and down trees. Bees fly from flower to flower, frogs leap, rabbits run, and fishes swim. Earthworms and ants work in their underground homes.

There are animals that turn colors, wear disguises, and light up parts of their bodies. And there are animals that dance, dig into rocks, and see colors we can't see. This book is about all kinds of animals: where they live, what they need, and how they stay alive.

Where Animals Live

Animals live all over the world. They live in oceans, rivers, and lakes. They live in deserts, forests, and caves. They live on mountains, plains, and seashores, even in freezing Antarctica. But no kind of animal can live in all these places. For example, a shark lives in water, where it can swim, breathe, and find food. A shark cannot live on land because its body is not fitted, or adapted, to life out of water. Camels, on the other hand, live in the desert and on plains. They can't live in water or at the North Pole.

What Animals Need

No matter where an animal lives, it needs food and water. Animals can't make their own food; only plants can. Plants make food using energy from the sun. Food contains the proteins, sugars, fats, vitamins, and minerals animals need to grow strong and healthy. Food also contains energy. Animals need energy to move and to keep their bodies working properly.

To get energy out of food, animals need the gas called oxygen. Oxygen is found in both air and water. Land animals get oxygen from the air. Most water animals get oxygen from the water. Every day, when plants make food, they also make oxygen, so that the supply never runs out.

Animal bodies are made up of cells. Nearly all cells are so tiny they can be seen only through a microscope. The smallest animals are made up of just one cell. But most animals have millions of cells in their bodies, all working together.

As cells work, they produce poisonous wastes. Animals get rid of these wastes before they can do any harm. One waste is the gas called carbon dioxide. It is very important because plants use it and water to make more food.

Some animals eat plants; others eat animals. Still others eat both plants and animals. An animal that kills another animal for food is called a predator. For instance, a mouse eats plants and insects. A hungry rattlesnake may eat the mouse. The snake is the predator and the mouse is its prey. If a hawk eats the rattlesnake, the hawk is the predator and the snake becomes the prey. When animals die from diseases, injuries, or old age, they also become food for other animals.

To stay alive, animals will defend themselves any way they can. They may try to run, jump, swim, fly, or hide from a predator. Or they may try to scare a predator away. And, if they have to, most animals will fight for their lives.

Groups of Animals

When animals become adults, they can reproduce. Cats have kittens, bears have cubs, and ducks have ducklings. As long as each kind of animal reproduces, it will not become extinct.

There are more than a million and a half kinds of animals living on the earth. Each different kind is called a species. Scientists sort all the different species into groups. All the animals in a group are alike in one or more ways.

The first part of this book is about the different groups of animals without bones in their bodies (invertebrates). Jellyfishes, snails, grasshoppers, worms, and lobsters are all invertebrates. The rest of the book is about animals with backbones (vertebrates), such as catfishes, toads, turtles, owls, kangaroos, lions, and giraffes.

At this very moment, some animals are hunting. Others are resting, building homes, or taking care of their young. Some animals are even playing. From the tiniest one-celled animal to the largest elephants and whales, all animals make up the animal world.

One-Celled Animals

THE SIMPLEST ANIMALS are made up of only one cell. They are called protozoa. Some protozoa are so tiny that 5,000 lined up in a row measure just 1 inch (2.5 centimeters). There are more than 30,000 species of protozoa. Because there are so many of each species, it is impossible to count them all.

Protozoa almost always have to live surrounded by liquid, or they dry out and die. Most live in oceans, rivers, and lakes. In the oceans, nearly all protozoa live close to one-celled plants, called algae. Algae don't have roots, stems, or leaves. But like all other plants, algae make their own food. Many protozoa eat algae or other one-celled animals.

Both one-celled plants and animals make up part of the plankton (page 44). Plankton is food for many ocean animals, including the blue whale, the largest animal.

Many protozoa live among the grains of sand on the beach. Others live among soil particles in the ground. In soil, some protozoa feed on the dead bodies of larger animals and plants. Along with other living things, they break the dead bodies apart. As they do this, they put useful substances back into the soil, water, and air. These substances are needed by other animals and plants.

A few kinds of protozoa live inside plants or larger animals. Sometimes the protozoa cause diseases, but mostly they are very helpful. For instance, protozoa living in a cow's stomach help the cow to digest the grass it eats.

When most one-celled animals have grown to a certain size, they divide in half. Each half is a new one-celled animal, complete with all the parts it needs to keep living and growing.

Like all animals, protozoa can protect themselves. Some have hard shells or glassy coverings around them. Others produce poison. If the weather gets too cold or dry, some protozoa give off a liquid to protect themselves. This liquid hardens around them into a covering, called a cyst. When the weather gets warmer or wetter, they break out of the cysts and become active.

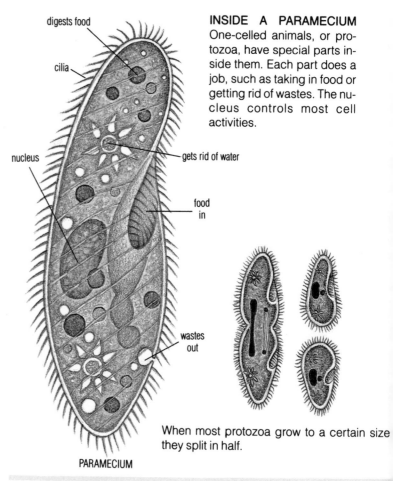

INSIDE A PARAMECIUM One-celled animals, or protozoa, have special parts inside them. Each part does a job, such as taking in food or getting rid of wastes. The nucleus controls most cell activities.

digests food

cilia

nucleus

gets rid of water

food in

wastes out

PARAMECIUM

When most protozoa grow to a certain size they split in half.

WHERE PROTOZOA LIVE

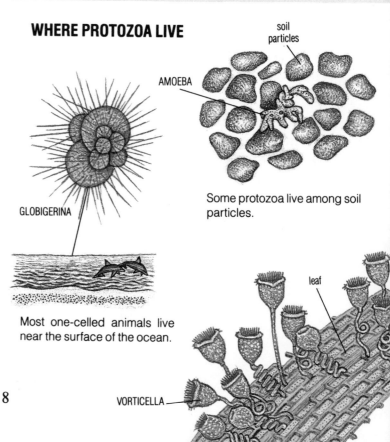

soil particles

AMOEBA

GLOBIGERINA

Some protozoa live among soil particles.

Most one-celled animals live near the surface of the ocean.

leaf

VORTICELLA

HOW PROTOZOA MOVE

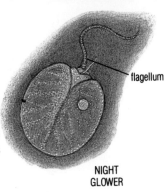

One-celled night glowers glow in the dark, lighting up the surface of ocean waters. To move, a night glower whips its flagellum back and forth.

NIGHT GLOWER

SPIROSTOMUM

By beating its cilia like oars, this one-celled animal moves through the water.

cilia

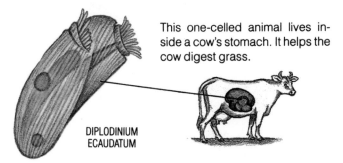

The amoeba's body changes shape as it flows along.

AMOEBA

This one-celled animal lives inside a cow's stomach. It helps the cow digest grass.

DIPLODINIUM ECAUDATUM

Some protozoa cause diseases. This one lives inside certain mosquitoes. It can cause malaria in some of the animals the mosquito bites.

PLASMODIUM

Many protozoa live in freshwater rivers, lakes, and streams. Fresh water has very little salt in it.

SELF-PROTECTION

Some protozoa have shells around them. When they die, their shells sink to the sea floor.

FORAMINIFERA

sand

Sand stuck to this one-celled animal protects it.

TINTINNOPSIS

FOOD FOR PROTOZOA

ALGA

STENTOR

Many protozoa eat algae (one-celled plants) floating in the water.

TERMITE PARASITE

This one-celled animal lives inside a termite's stomach and digests wood the termite swallows (page 41).

wood

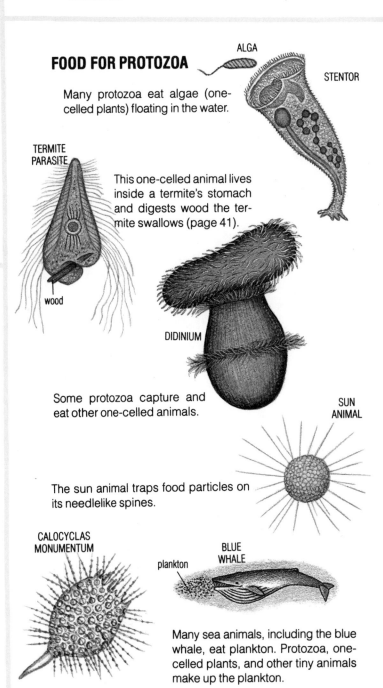

DIDINIUM

Some protozoa capture and eat other one-celled animals.

SUN ANIMAL

The sun animal traps food particles on its needlelike spines.

CALOCYCLAS MONUMENTUM

BLUE WHALE

plankton

Many sea animals, including the blue whale, eat plankton. Protozoa, one-celled plants, and other tiny animals make up the plankton.

Sponges

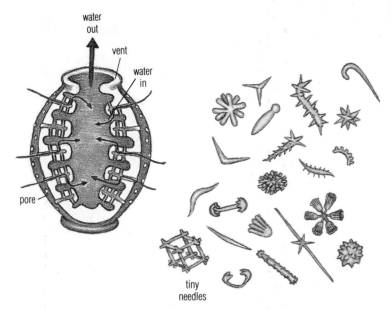

INSIDE A SPONGE A sponge's body is made up of two layers of cells with a jelly in between. Many sponges have hard, tiny needles in this jelly. As shown, these needles, or spicules, have many shapes in different sponges. Sponges get food and oxygen from the water they take into their pores.

SPONGES ARE ANIMALS, not plants. Most live in shallow ocean waters all over the world. Just a few species of sponges live in freshwater lakes, rivers, and ponds. There are more than 10,000 species of sponges. Some are shaped like vases, others like cups, fans, tubes, and funnels.

Sponges don't have heads, hearts, or stomachs. Their simple bodies are made up of only two layers of cells. In between these layers is a clear jelly in which special cells wander.

On the outside of a sponge's body are tiny openings called pores. Except when they are resting, sponges pull water into their pores. From the water, sponge cells trap food particles and remove oxygen. The sponge cells also release wastes into the water. When the sponge pumps the water out of a large opening called a vent, the water carries the wastes away.

For support and protection, most sponges have a skeleton in their jelly layer. Sponge skeletons are not made of bones. Some are made of tiny needles that are as hard as stone or glass. Other sponge skeletons are soft and elastic.

Almost all sponges reproduce by using egg cells and sperm cells. The egg cells stay inside the sponge's body, but the sperm cells are released into the water. Many of the sperm cells are pulled into other sponges. When one sperm cell joins with one egg cell, the egg cell becomes fertilized. This means that it can now develop into a new sponge.

A new sponge is tiny. It is called a larva, and it doesn't look like an adult sponge. The tiny sponge larva swims for a day or two. Then it settles to the ocean floor and attaches itself to a rock or a shell. There it lives its entire life. Slowly the larva's body grows and changes into an adult sponge.

Sponges can also reproduce without sperm and egg cells. To do this, part of a sponge's body buds out, breaks off, and grows into a new sponge.

Very few animals eat sponges because they don't taste good. But a lot of animals, including some small crabs and fishes, find safety hiding inside a sponge.

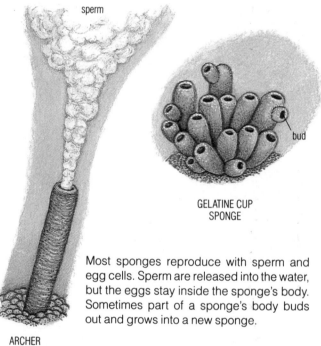

GELATINE CUP SPONGE

ARCHER SPONGE

Most sponges reproduce with sperm and egg cells. Sperm are released into the water, but the eggs stay inside the sponge's body. Sometimes part of a sponge's body buds out and grows into a new sponge.

There are four main groups of sponges. The fire sponge (a), glass sponge (b), coralline cave sponge (c), and encrusting sponge (d) each belong to one of these different groups.

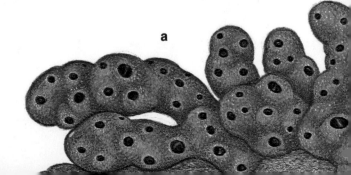

10

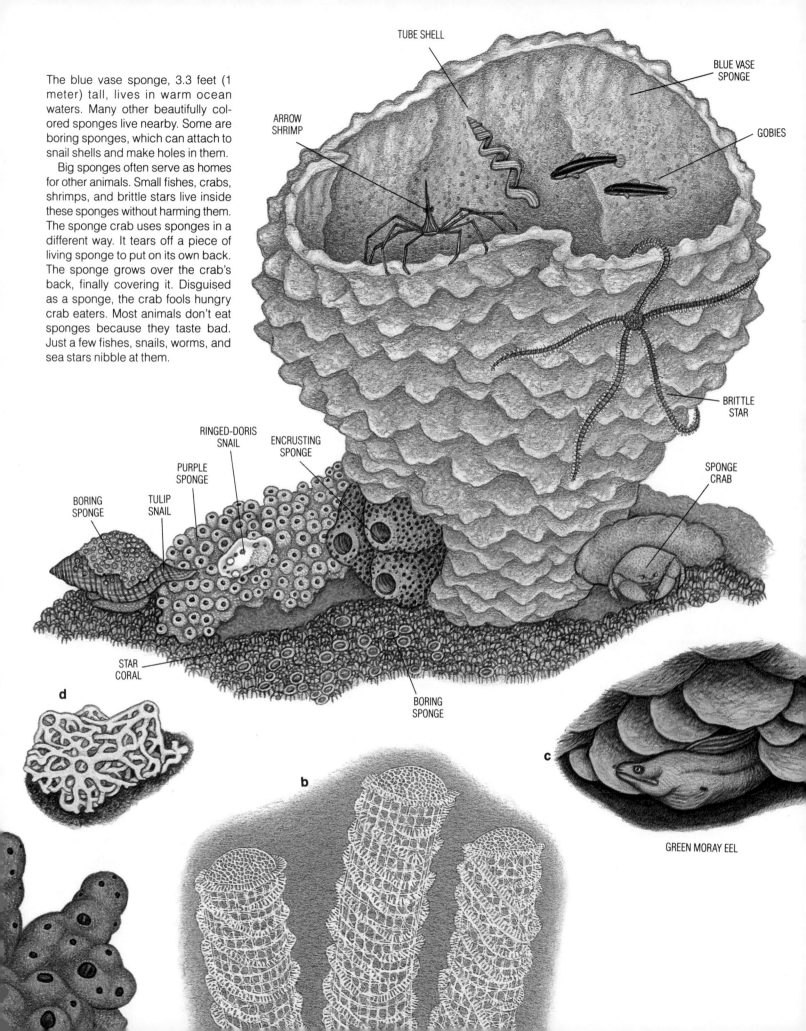

The blue vase sponge, 3.3 feet (1 meter) tall, lives in warm ocean waters. Many other beautifully colored sponges live nearby. Some are boring sponges, which can attach to snail shells and make holes in them.

Big sponges often serve as homes for other animals. Small fishes, crabs, shrimps, and brittle stars live inside these sponges without harming them. The sponge crab uses sponges in a different way. It tears off a piece of living sponge to put on its own back. The sponge grows over the crab's back, finally covering it. Disguised as a sponge, the crab fools hungry crab eaters. Most animals don't eat sponges because they taste bad. Just a few fishes, snails, worms, and sea stars nibble at them.

TUBE SHELL

BLUE VASE SPONGE

ARROW SHRIMP

GOBIES

BRITTLE STAR

SPONGE CRAB

RINGED-DORIS SNAIL

ENCRUSTING SPONGE

PURPLE SPONGE

BORING SPONGE

TULIP SNAIL

STAR CORAL

BORING SPONGE

d

b

c

GREEN MORAY EEL

Stinging-Cell Animals

Some of the most beautiful animals living in the oceans are jellyfishes. They swim about, opening and closing their umbrella-shaped bodies. A jellyfish's body is made up of two layers of cells with a thick, light, colorless jelly in between. Underneath, in the center of the jellyfish's body, is its mouth. Almost always, feelers called tentacles surround the mouth. Some jellyfishes have tentacles that grow to be 100 feet (33 m) long.

Many jellyfishes use their tentacles to capture small fishes, shrimps, and crabs. The tentacles are armed with special stinging cells that explode open and shoot out hooked threads like harpoons. Some of these threads entangle prey. Others inject a paralyzing poison, making it easier for the tentacles to capture the prey.

As they swim, jellyfishes depend on their tentacles for protection. In spite of these poisonous tentacles, some fishes, turtles, and birds eat jellyfishes.

Although a few jellyfishes can't swim, nearly all the rest swim for most of their lives. Their simple muscles and nerves help control their movements. Jellyfishes don't have brains, but many have simple eyes that can see light and so detect when the sun is shining. Jellyfishes also have cells that distinguish up from down. This is important because most jellyfishes will die if they sink too deep into the dark ocean waters, where there is no food for them. Since jellyfishes can't live on land, they will die in the sand or mud if the water carries them ashore.

There are male jellyfishes and female jellyfishes. The males produce sperm cells and the females egg cells. The illustration at the right shows some of the changes a jellyfish goes through during its life.

There are about 10,000 other species of animals that also have tentacles with stinging cells in them. Some of these are the brightly colored sea anemones, sea fans, sea pens, and sea pansies. Instead of swimming or drifting, these animals spend most of their lives attached to rocks and shells or in the sand and mud.

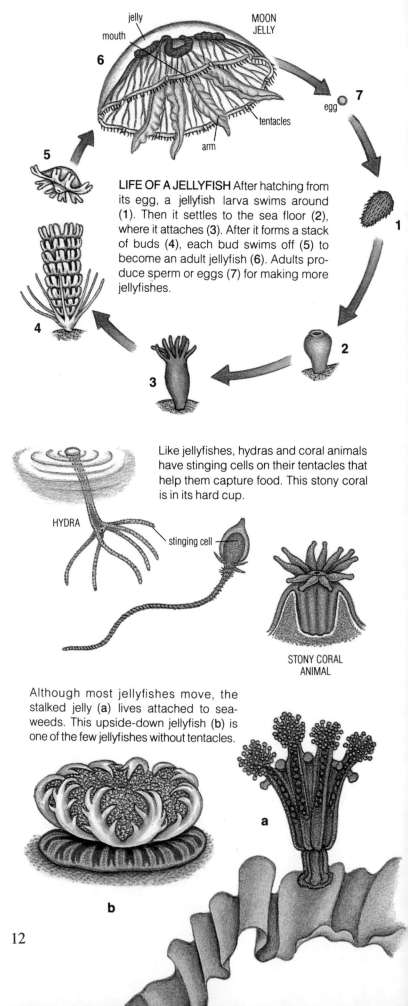

LIFE OF A JELLYFISH After hatching from its egg, a jellyfish larva swims around (1). Then it settles to the sea floor (2), where it attaches (3). After it forms a stack of buds (4), each bud swims off (5) to become an adult jellyfish (6). Adults produce sperm or eggs (7) for making more jellyfishes.

Like jellyfishes, hydras and coral animals have stinging cells on their tentacles that help them capture food. This stony coral is in its hard cup.

Although most jellyfishes move, the stalked jelly (a) lives attached to seaweeds. This upside-down jellyfish (b) is one of the few jellyfishes without tentacles.

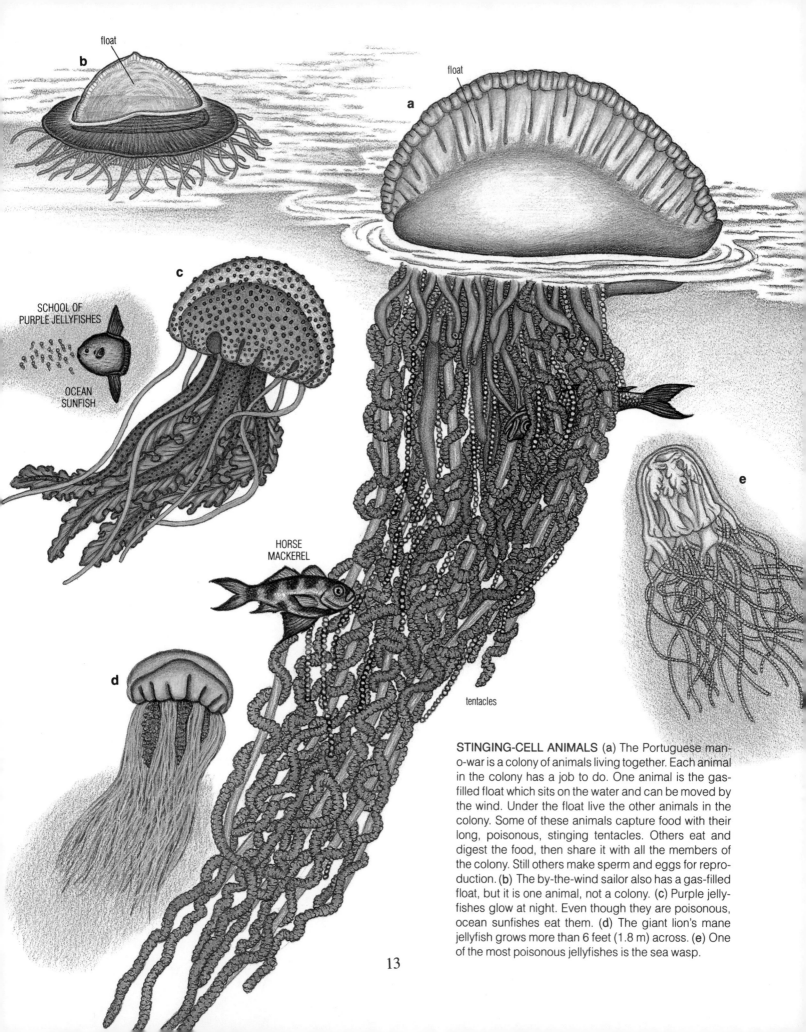

float

b

float

a

c

SCHOOL OF
PURPLE JELLYFISHES

OCEAN
SUNFISH

HORSE
MACKEREL

d

e

tentacles

STINGING-CELL ANIMALS (a) The Portuguese man-o-war is a colony of animals living together. Each animal in the colony has a job to do. One animal is the gas-filled float which sits on the water and can be moved by the wind. Under the float live the other animals in the colony. Some of these animals capture food with their long, poisonous, stinging tentacles. Others eat and digest the food, then share it with all the members of the colony. Still others make sperm and eggs for repro-duction. (b) The by-the-wind sailor also has a gas-filled float, but it is one animal, not a colony. (c) Purple jelly-fishes glow at night. Even though they are poisonous, ocean sunfishes eat them. (d) The giant lion's mane jellyfish grows more than 6 feet (1.8 m) across. (e) One of the most poisonous jellyfishes is the sea wasp.

13

Some live alone, but others, like the corals, live together in large colonies.

Most stony corals are tiny animals. As they grow, their soft bodies give off a limy substance that hardens around them into chalky cups. These protective cups are skeletons on the outside of their bodies. Each coral is attached to its cup and can't swim out of it. During the day, most species of stony corals hide in their cups with their tentacles curled in over them. This makes it very difficult for coral eaters to get at them. At night, the corals open like flowers, stretch out their tentacles, and catch small sea animals as they swim by.

When corals reproduce, they start their own colonies. In a colony, one coral is connected to another. As each kind of coral colony slowly grows larger and larger, it takes on its own shape. Some are as flat as tables; others look like trees or antlers.

Coral Reefs

In the sea, many species of corals build up huge walls, called reefs. Reef-building corals have to live in clear, sunlit, shallow ocean waters where the temperature is warm all year round. Almost always, algae live inside these corals, making oxygen and some of the food the corals need.

When corals die, their stony cups remain and new

ON A CORAL REEF Billions of tiny coral animals build up great undersea walls called reefs. Each coral lives in a hard, chalky cup. During the day most corals hide in their cups. At night they open their stinging tentacles to capture food. When they die, their cups remain and new corals build new cups on top of the old ones.

Other animals with stinging tentacles live on this coral reef: sea anemones, sea fans, sea whips, and soft corals. Brightly colored fishes, crabs, sponges, and snails also live on the reef because they can

VENUS SEA FAN

BLUE CHROMIS FISH

CLOWN FISH

GURNEY'S SEA PEN

SEA PANSY

ARMORED SEA STAR

GIANT ANEMONE

corals build cups right on top of them. Very, very slowly, over hundreds of thousands of years, billions of corals build so many cups on top of each other that great coral walls rise up from the ocean floor. As the walls spread out they take on unusual shapes, forming ledges and caves. The largest coral reef, the Great Barrier Reef, off the coast of Australia, is more than 1,250 miles (2,000 kilometers) long and more than 95 miles (152 km) wide.

Many different kinds of plants and animals live on coral reefs, which provide them with lots of sunlight, many places to hide and grow, and plenty of food to eat. Some of these reef animals are bright-colored, striped, and spotted fishes; crabs; giant clams; sponges; snails; and sea anemones. Other kinds of corals, which have tough, leathery skeletons instead of stony ones, live there too. Sea turtles and some fishes visit reefs in search of food.

Most animals that live on reefs don't harm them. But some, such as the crown-of-thorns sea star and the parrot fish, eat corals and damage reefs. Polluted water also damages coral reefs.

By building reefs, the tiny corals transform their surroundings into one of the most varied and colorful parts of the animal world.

find food to eat and places to hide. Most fishes have to avoid the fatal stings of the sea anemone's tentacles. Clown fishes, though, are not harmed by these tentacles and can swim safely among them. When sea anemones sense danger, they pull in their tentacles.

Most reef animals don't harm corals, but some bristle worms, the parrot fish, and the crown-of-thorns sea star eat them.

Although a sea pen and sea pansies are shown here, they do not live on coral reefs.

ELKHORN CORAL

STAGHORN CORAL

BRAIN CORAL

SEA ROD

FLOWER CORAL

ROUND STARLET CORAL

YELLOW SPONGE

CROWN OF THORNS

BOULDER CORAL

PARROT FISH

BEADLET ANEMONE

SOME UNUSUAL ANIMALS

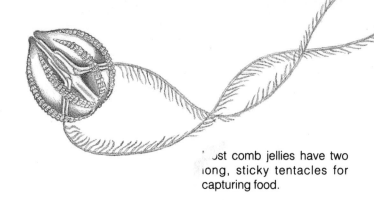

EIGHTEEN DIFFERENT ANIMAL species are shown on these two pages. Each species stands for a whole group of animals similar to it. Together, all of the groups total more than 100,000 species of the most unusual animals in the animal world.

Most comb jellies have two long, sticky tentacles for capturing food.

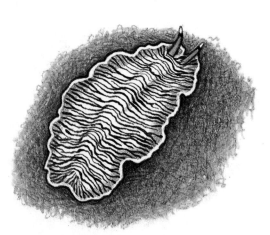

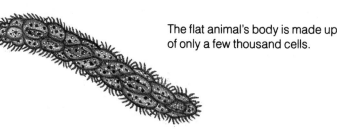

The flat animal's body is made up of only a few thousand cells.

Some middle animals live inside the bodies of squids and octopuses.

There are more than 15,000 species of flat-worms. This one is crawling over pebbles on the sea floor. If part of a flatworm's body is ripped off, it will grow back.

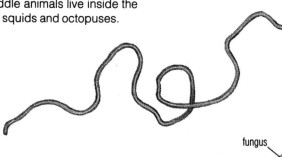

fungus

More than 80,000 species of round-worms live in oceans, lakes, and moist soils and inside plants and other animals. This roundworm is trapped by a fungus in the soil. (A fungus is not an animal.)

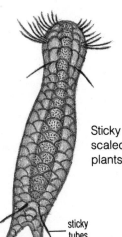

Sticky tubes on their bodies help scaled animals cling to water plants and rocks.

sticky tubes

Some ribbon worms grow to be less than 1 inch (2.5 cm) long. Others grow to be more than 90 feet (27 m) long. This 2-inch (5-cm) ribbon worm has caught another kind of worm to eat.

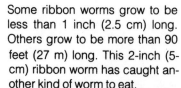

Tiny jaw-mouthed worms swim, twist, and move their heads from side to side.

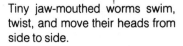

16

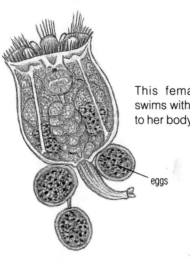

This female wheel animal swims with her eggs attached to her body.

eggs

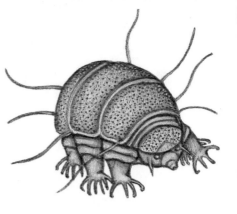

If a water bear dries up, it doesn't die. Instead, it shrinks and waits for rain. Then it returns to its normal size and starts moving again.

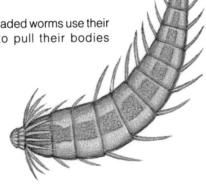

Spiny-headed worms use their snouts to pull their bodies along.

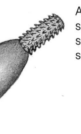

One female horsehair worm can lay millions of eggs and wrap them around water plants.

Most stalked animals live together in colonies attached to rocks or shells.

All thorny-headed worms live inside the bodies of other animals, such as dogs, pigs, rats, and seals.

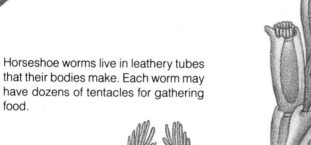

Nearly all of the 3,000 species of moss animals live in the sea. Some colonies of moss animals resemble moss or seaweed.

Horseshoe worms live in leathery tubes that their bodies make. Each worm may have dozens of tentacles for gathering food.

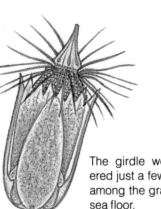

The girdle wearer was discovered just a few years ago. It lives among the grains of sand on the sea floor.

When a lampshell opens its shells, it gathers food with its tentacles.

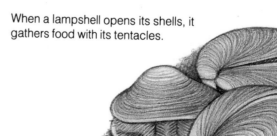

Mollusks

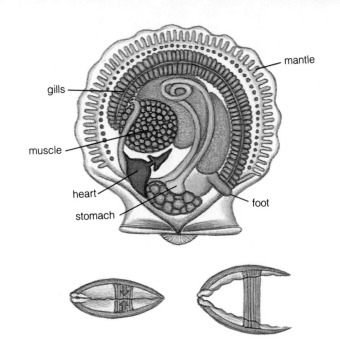

E VERY DAY, MILLIONS OF empty shells wash up on shores all over the world. Inside these shells once lived animals, called mollusks, with soft, boneless bodies. There are more than 100,000 species of mollusks, and about 80,000 of them are snails. Oysters, clams, octopuses, and squids are some of the others. Whereas the smallest mollusks can hardly be seen without a microscope, the largest, the giant squid, can grow to more than 60 feet (18 m) long. It is the largest boneless animal in the animal world.

Most mollusks live in the ocean. Some live on the seashore, in trees, and even high up in the mountains. To breathe, almost all ocean mollusks use their gills to take oxygen out of the water. Land mollusks breathe through lungs, which take oxygen out of the air.

Soft mollusk bodies are made up of many layers and different kinds of cells. These cells form organs such as gills, kidneys, the heart, and the stomach. Each organ has jobs to do, and all the organs work together to keep each animal alive and healthy.

Mollusks have a thin skin called a mantle. Its job is to make a shell. The mantle gives off limy substances that harden into a shell when they come in contact with water or air. Many shells have three layers, making them strong enough to serve as shields against attack by hungry animals. Usually, the outer layer is rough, hard, and thick. The middle layer is chalky, and the inner layer is smooth and sometimes pearly. As shells form they take on many different shapes, patterns, and colors.

Most mollusks make their shells on the outside of their bodies. As these animals grow, their shells keep growing too. Some mollusks don't have shells outside their bodies. Instead, they have a small shell inside them. There are even some mollusks that lose their shells as they become adults.

SNAILS

Snails are mollusks that live in a coiled shell that they carry on their backs. When danger is near, most snails pull their bodies into their shells for safety. Some snails, called slugs, have little or no shell.

INSIDE A SCALLOP Scallops are mollusks that live within two hard shells. Their soft bodies are made up of many organs. Each organ does different work: the heart pumps blood, the mantle makes the shell, and the gills take in oxygen and gather food particles. A muscle pulls the scallop's two shells tightly together.

A chiton's shell is made of eight overlapping plates (**a**). Its strong, muscular foot can cling tightly to rocks (**b**). When a chiton is frightened, it can curl up into a ball (**c**).

CHITON

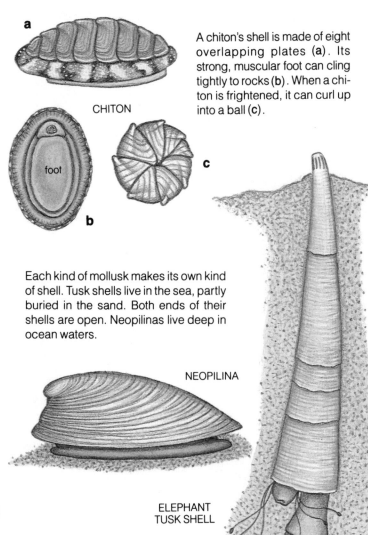

Each kind of mollusk makes its own kind of shell. Tusk shells live in the sea, partly buried in the sand. Both ends of their shells are open. Neopilinas live deep in ocean waters.

NEOPILINA

ELEPHANT TUSK SHELL

SHORE LIFE Many mollusks live on the seashore. They spend part of each day underwater and part of each day exposed to the air. At high tide (shown here), when they are covered by seawater, mollusks capture food and get oxygen from the water.

But everything changes when the tide goes out, for these animals are left behind in the open air. Now they have to protect their soft bodies from strong winds, dry air, hot and cold temperatures, and hungry shorebirds. Most close themselves up inside their shells. To keep moist, they seal in some seawater with them. Snails, mussels, and chitons cling to rocks so that they won't be pulled away by pounding waves or predators. Clams stay buried in the cool, moist sand. When the tide returns, these mollusks continue their underwater life.

Not all shore animals are mollusks. Some, such as sponges, anemones, moss animals, lampshells, and horseshoe worms, are shown here too.

high tide

YELLOW PERIWINKLE SNAIL

EDIBLE MUSSEL

RED CHITON

KEYHOLE LIMPET

STRAWBERRY ANEMONE

MOSS ANIMALS

HORSESHOE WORM

BREADCRUMB SPONGE

RED ABALONE SNAIL

low tide

LIGHTNING WHELK SNAIL

STOUT JACKKNIFE CLAM

LAMPSHELLS

EDIBLE COCKLE

SNAILS With more than 80,000 species, snails make up the largest group of mollusks, the gastropods. Most snails live in spiral shells, which protect their soft bodies. Some snails, called slugs, have little or no shell. Snails have eyes, tentacles on their heads, and a filelike tongue called a radula. They also have a flat, muscular foot. Most snails use their foot for creeping. Some also use it for digging in sand or for clinging to rocks.

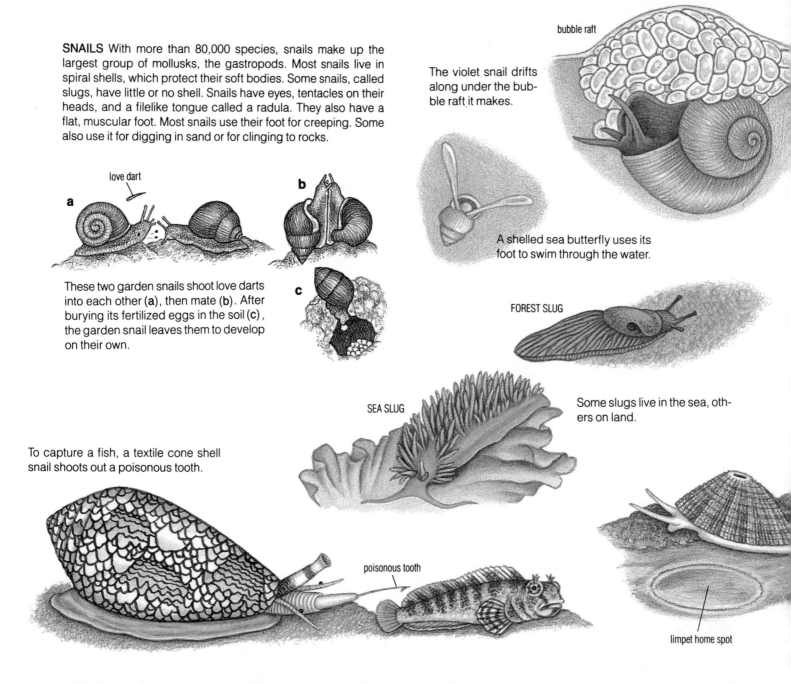

love dart

a

b

c

These two garden snails shoot love darts into each other (**a**), then mate (**b**). After burying its fertilized eggs in the soil (**c**), the garden snail leaves them to develop on their own.

bubble raft

The violet snail drifts along under the bubble raft it makes.

A shelled sea butterfly uses its foot to swim through the water.

FOREST SLUG

Some slugs live in the sea, others on land.

SEA SLUG

To capture a fish, a textile cone shell snail shoots out a poisonous tooth.

poisonous tooth

limpet home spot

Below their stomachs, snails have a muscular foot, on which they creep slowly about. As snails move, they give off a slimy mucus that makes it easier for their foot to slide along smoothly. In an hour, some snails move less than 10 feet (3 m). Many snails also use their foot to dig into the sand or mud. Others use their foot to cling to rocks.

On a snail's head are its eyes and its tentacles, for feeling and smelling. Almost all snails have a filelike tongue, called a radula. It is covered with rows of tiny teeth made of a tough substance called chitin. Like a file, the radula scrapes, cuts, tears, and grinds the food

a snail eats. Many snails eat plants or animals, such as earthworms and small fishes. Some snails can drill holes into the shells of other mollusks. Then, using their tubelike proboscis, they suck out the animal living in the shell.

Snails live almost everywhere: in soil, caves, trees, jungles, forests, deserts, fresh waters, and all the oceans. No matter where they live, they have to watch out for the birds, frogs, snakes, fishes, and mice that eat them.

During the hot part of the day, land snails may find cool, damp, safe places to rest. To hide, some snails

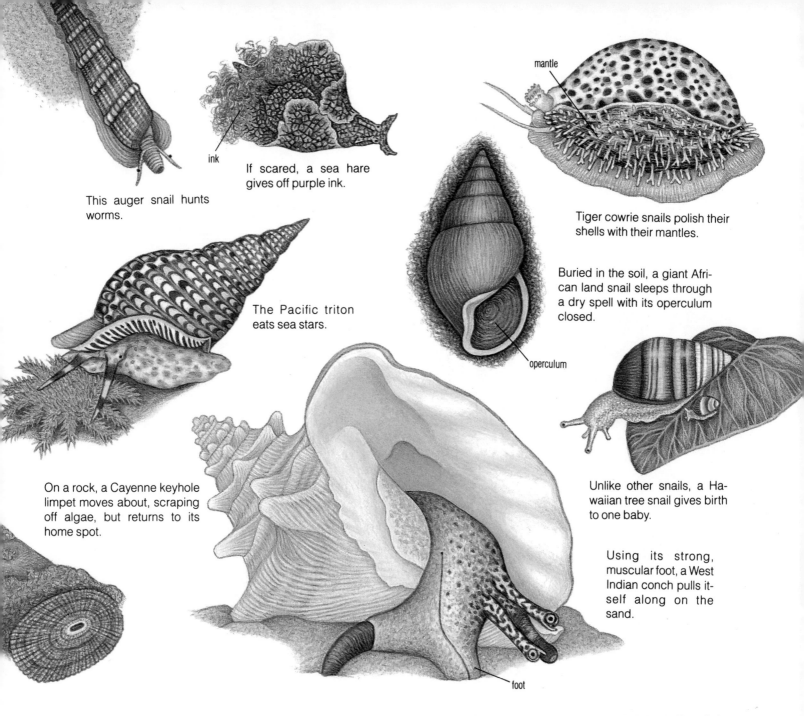

This auger snail hunts worms.

ink

If scared, a sea hare gives off purple ink.

mantle

Tiger cowrie snails polish their shells with their mantles.

The Pacific triton eats sea stars.

Buried in the soil, a giant African land snail sleeps through a dry spell with its operculum closed.

operculum

On a rock, a Cayenne keyhole limpet moves about, scraping off algae, but returns to its home spot.

Unlike other snails, a Hawaiian tree snail gives birth to one baby.

Using its strong, muscular foot, a West Indian conch pulls itself along on the sand.

foot

cover their bodies with leaves. Others stay on rocks or leaves where their body colors blend in with the background colors. By camouflaging themselves in this way, these snails make themselves less easy to find. Later, in the cool of the night, they come out to feed.

In autumn, land snails usually bury themselves under the ground and seal themselves tightly in their shells so that they won't dry out. They hibernate, or sleep, through winter until the spring rains come and the weather gets warmer. In summer, they may also sleep buried underground if the weather gets too hot or dry.

Before they can reproduce, two land snails of the same species must find each other. When they do, they sometimes signal that they are ready to mate. Snails' courtship signals consist of circling around each other and touching tentacles.

In most land and water snails, sperm cells join with egg cells inside the snail's body. The fertilized eggs are then released into water or buried in soil. Almost all snails abandon their eggs and never see their babies. When a land snail hatches from its egg, it looks like its parents except that it is tiny. Newly hatched water snails are wormlike. As they mature, they change

TWO-SHELLED MOLLUSKS Clams, oysters, scallops, and mussels live between two shells. Many animals try to pry open these shells and eat the soft mollusks inside. Sea stars work hard to pull the shells apart, and some snails drill holes in them. Two-shelled mollusks are also known as bivalves.

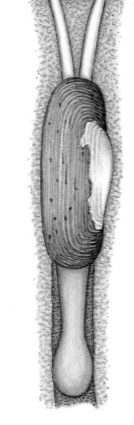

siphon tubes

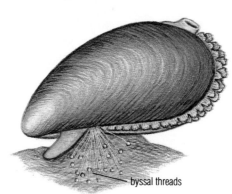

Common shipworms tunnel into wood but rock borers dig into rocks.

Buried in the sand, a stout jackknife razor clam takes in water through one siphon tube. Once its gills remove oxygen and food from the water, the clam expels the water through another tube.

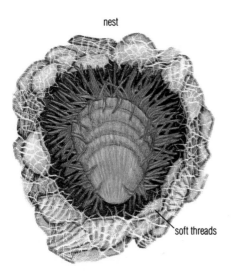

nest

soft threads

A file shell builds a nest of rocks and shell pieces. Then it lines the nest with soft threads it makes.

byssal threads

Edible mussels produce tough byssal threads which attach securely to rocks.

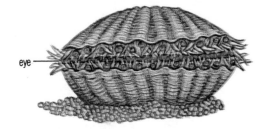

When danger is near, the leafy jewel box shuts its shells.

Most mussels live in the sea, but this freshwater mussel lives in rivers and lakes.

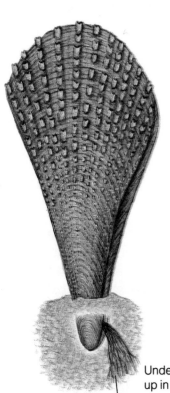

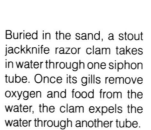

This giant scallop's blue eyes warn it when to close its shells.

eye

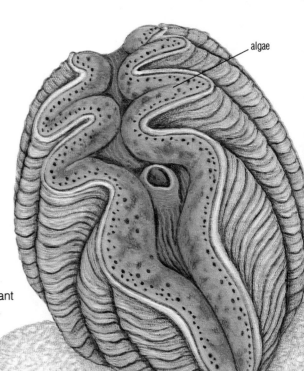

algae

Underwater, pen shells stand up in the sand.

byssal threads

Algae grow inside this giant clam, 4 feet (1.2 m) long.

to look like their parents. Although one snail can lay hundreds or thousands of eggs, most young snails die or are eaten before they grow up. Even so, some snails live more than 15 years.

TWO-SHELLED MOLLUSKS

More than 15,000 mollusk species, including all clams, scallops, mussels, and oysters, live within two shells. A hinge holds the two shells together, and powerful muscles keep them tightly shut when the animal inside senses danger.

Unlike snails, two-shelled mollusks don't have a head or a radula tongue. Their large gills not only take oxygen from the water but also filter out tiny water plants and animals as food.

Some two-shelled mollusks spend most of their lives in one place. Many clams, for instance, use their ax-shaped foot to dig themselves an underground hole, or burrow, in soft mud or sand. Mussels give off tough byssal threads, which attach securely to rocks.

Other two-shelled mollusks live on the sea floor and move around. When scallops, for example, want to escape from danger, they can clap their shells together and zigzag away through the water.

Every day, two-shelled mollusks face many dangers. Hungry sea stars attack them, trying to pry open their shells. Some snails slowly drill holes in their shells. Oyster-catcher birds hammer them open, and walruses dig them out of the sand. Despite all such threats, with their two shells tightly shut these mollusks have some of the best protection to be found in the animal world.

CEPHALOPODS

Darting about in the oceans are squids, octopuses, cuttlefishes, and nautiluses. These amazing mollusks are called cephalopods. Instead of having a foot, they all have at least eight powerful arms surrounding their mouth. Often their arms have suckers on them, which help catch food or grip to rocks and other objects.

Among the cephalopods only the nautilus grows a shell on the outside of its body. The shell is divided into chambers. The nautilus lives in the largest chamber. When it grows too big for that chamber, it just

Walruses dig for buried clams.

23

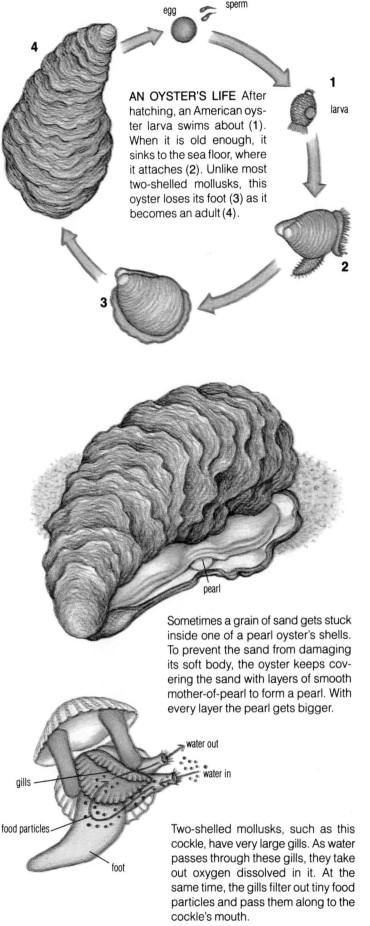

AN OYSTER'S LIFE After hatching, an American oyster larva swims about (1). When it is old enough, it sinks to the sea floor, where it attaches (2). Unlike most two-shelled mollusks, this oyster loses its foot (3) as it becomes an adult (4).

egg   sperm

1   larva

2

3

4

pearl

Sometimes a grain of sand gets stuck inside one of a pearl oyster's shells. To prevent the sand from damaging its soft body, the oyster keeps covering the sand with layers of smooth mother-of-pearl to form a pearl. With every layer the pearl gets bigger.

water out

water in

gills

food particles

foot

Two-shelled mollusks, such as this cockle, have very large gills. As water passes through these gills, they take out oxygen dissolved in it. At the same time, the gills filter out tiny food particles and pass them along to the cockle's mouth.

adds on a larger one to live in. The nautilus still uses its old chambers. It can fill them with a light gas that makes swimming easier.

Squids and cuttlefishes have some shell inside their bodies, but none on the outside. Both are excellent swimmers, hovering and cruising about in the water. When they swim, they shoot water jets out of their bodies through a special funnel. To move forward they shoot the water jets backward; to move up they shoot the water down.

Octopuses are the only mollusks that don't have any shell. Although they can swim, they usually just crawl over rocks and sand on the ocean floor, moving their soft, rubbery, baglike bodies along.

When cuttlefishes, squids, and octopuses hunt, they strike quickly to catch their favorite foods: shrimps, crabs, and fishes. With their strong beaks and filelike tongues, they bite and tear at their prey. Some also release a deadly nerve poison when they bite.

One of the remarkable things octopuses, squids, and cuttlefishes can do is change their body colors to match the colors of rocks and sand. As their colors

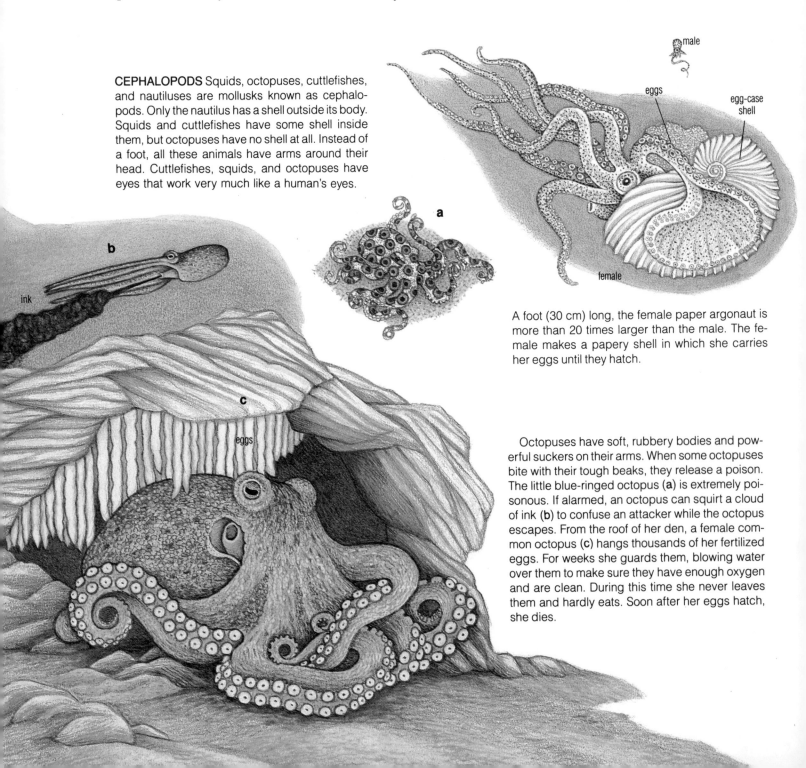

CEPHALOPODS Squids, octopuses, cuttlefishes, and nautiluses are mollusks known as cephalopods. Only the nautilus has a shell outside its body. Squids and cuttlefishes have some shell inside them, but octopuses have no shell at all. Instead of a foot, all these animals have arms around their head. Cuttlefishes, squids, and octopuses have eyes that work very much like a human's eyes.

A foot (30 cm) long, the female paper argonaut is more than 20 times larger than the male. The female makes a papery shell in which she carries her eggs until they hatch.

Octopuses have soft, rubbery bodies and powerful suckers on their arms. When some octopuses bite with their tough beaks, they release a poison. The little blue-ringed octopus (**a**) is extremely poisonous. If alarmed, an octopus can squirt a cloud of ink (**b**) to confuse an attacker while the octopus escapes. From the roof of her den, a female common octopus (**c**) hangs thousands of her fertilized eggs. For weeks she guards them, blowing water over them to make sure they have enough oxygen and are clean. During this time she never leaves them and hardly eats. Soon after her eggs hatch, she dies.

change, these animals blend into the world around them until they seem to disappear. Not only can they now ambush their prey without being seen, but other hungry animals can't find them because they are so well hidden.

When squids, octopuses, and cuttlefishes are alarmed or attacked by a predator, they can squirt a cloud of ink into the water. The ink cloud surprises and confuses a predator long enough for these clever animals to speed away through the water to safety.

When some octopuses mate, the male octopus sends courtship signals to the female by lifting his arms and changing color. When he senses the female is ready to mate, he rolls his sperm into a packet and places the packet inside the female's mantle cavity with one of his arms. Then the female retreats to her den, where she hangs thousands of her fertilized eggs from the roof. During the weeks it takes for her eggs to hatch, she never leaves them, not even to get food. Soon after the tiny octopuses hatch, she dies. The young octopuses that live grow up into some of the most intelligent of all sea animals.

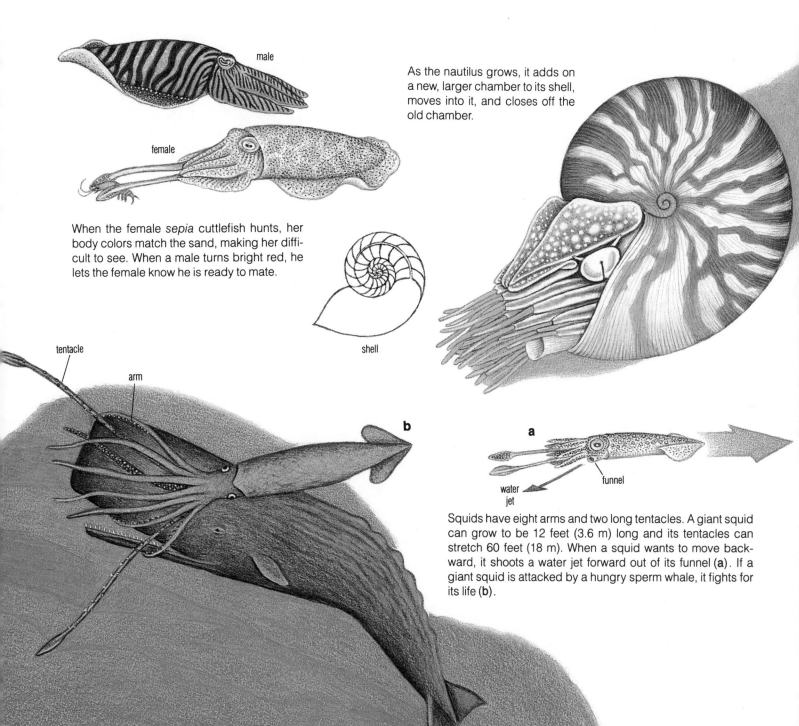

male

female

When the female *sepia* cuttlefish hunts, her body colors match the sand, making her difficult to see. When a male turns bright red, he lets the female know he is ready to mate.

shell

As the nautilus grows, it adds on a new, larger chamber to its shell, moves into it, and closes off the old chamber.

tentacle

arm

b

a

funnel

water jet

Squids have eight arms and two long tentacles. A giant squid can grow to be 12 feet (3.6 m) long and its tentacles can stretch 60 feet (18 m). When a squid wants to move backward, it shoots a water jet forward out of its funnel (**a**). If a giant squid is attacked by a hungry sperm whale, it fights for its life (**b**).

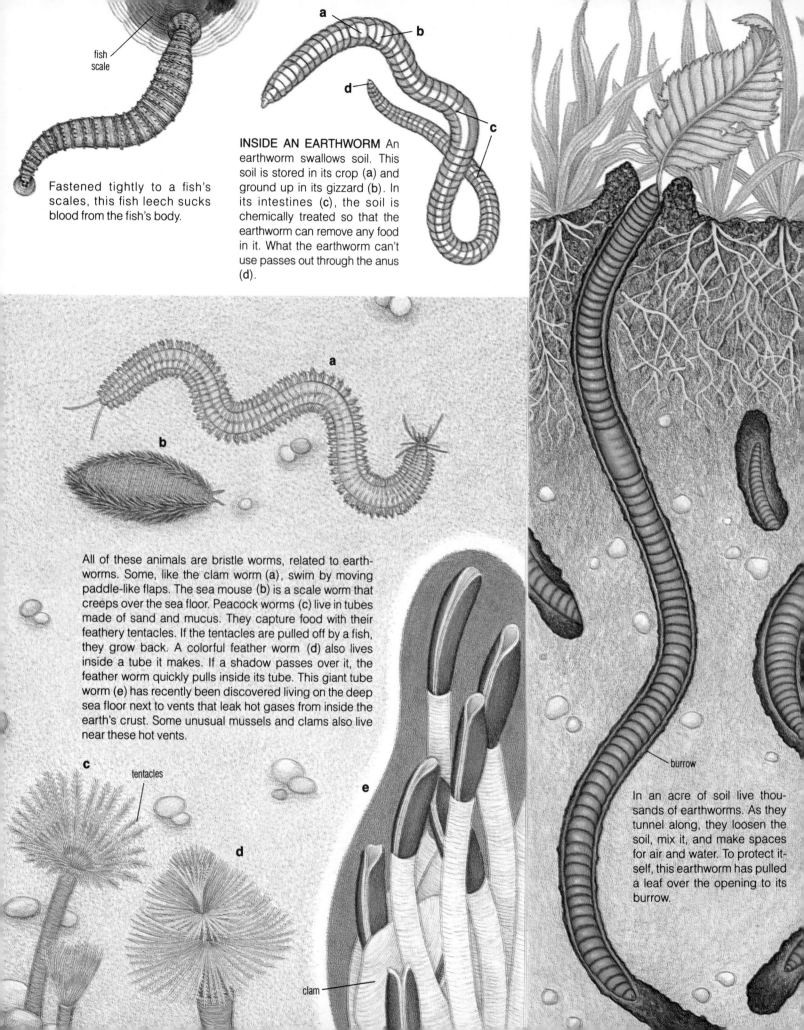

fish scale

Fastened tightly to a fish's scales, this fish leech sucks blood from the fish's body.

INSIDE AN EARTHWORM An earthworm swallows soil. This soil is stored in its crop (a) and ground up in its gizzard (b). In its intestines (c), the soil is chemically treated so that the earthworm can remove any food in it. What the earthworm can't use passes out through the anus (d).

All of these animals are bristle worms, related to earthworms. Some, like the clam worm (a), swim by moving paddle-like flaps. The sea mouse (b) is a scale worm that creeps over the sea floor. Peacock worms (c) live in tubes made of sand and mucus. They capture food with their feathery tentacles. If the tentacles are pulled off by a fish, they grow back. A colorful feather worm (d) also lives inside a tube it makes. If a shadow passes over it, the feather worm quickly pulls inside its tube. This giant tube worm (e) has recently been discovered living on the deep sea floor next to vents that leak hot gases from inside the earth's crust. Some unusual mussels and clams also live near these hot vents.

tentacles

clam

burrow

In an acre of soil live thousands of earthworms. As they tunnel along, they loosen the soil, mix it, and make spaces for air and water. To protect itself, this earthworm has pulled a leaf over the opening to its burrow.

Worms

HIDDEN IN SOILS all over the world are active earthworms. Billions of them burrow underground, tunneling along. They loosen and mix the soil constantly, creating spaces for air and water.

Earthworms not only tunnel through soil; they eat it too. The eaten soil passes through the earthworm's long food canal. The food canal removes any plant or animal food from it. By the time the soil reaches the end of the canal, it is ground down very fine and is ready to be released out the back end of the earthworm's body. With part of this soil the earthworm lines its burrow. The remainder the earthworm pushes up to the surface of the ground. Plants grow very well in this rich, fine soil deposited by earthworms. Since all animals depend on plants for food and oxygen, they rely on earthworms to take good care of the soil.

During the day earthworms stay out of the heat and light by remaining in their burrows. At night, though, many kinds crawl out in search of fallen leaves and flowers, which they drag back to their homes. Just in case danger is near, these earthworms usually keep their tail ends in their burrows. Often, for protection, earthworms barricade their burrow openings with leaves. Still, birds such as robins may pull earthworms from their burrows and eat them.

Earthworms have no arms, legs, teeth, jaws, nose, or eyes. Their bodies are divided into more than a hundred ringlike sections. Inside, instead of bones there is fluid. When an earthworm's strong muscles push against this fluid, they can make the earthworm's body shorter and thicker or longer and thinner. Stiff, short bristles stick out through the skin, gripping and anchoring an earthworm's body as it moves.

From the air trapped in soil, earthworms take oxygen in through their thin, moist skin. If earthworms dry out, they die. In winter or when the soil dries up, earthworms tunnel deep, make a chamber, and line the chamber with mucus that hardens. There they remain rolled up, not moving until the soil becomes wet.

There are more than 8,000 other species of worms that also have bodies divided into sections. Many, like the bristle worms, live in the oceans inside tubes that they build.

OTHER WORMS Each of these worms stands for an entire group. Most live in the oceans. (a) There are only a few species of cucumber worms. (b) Arrow worms flap their tails to move forward and backward. (c) Most peanut worms dig burrows. (d) Long, thin beard worms live in tubes. (e) Most acorn worms live alone. (f) Like an innkeeper, this spoon worm shares its home with a small clam, fish, and crab. (g) Tongue worms live inside animals such as snakes and foxes. (h) Velvet worms live in the forest. During the winter they stay in their burrows, protected from snow and cold.

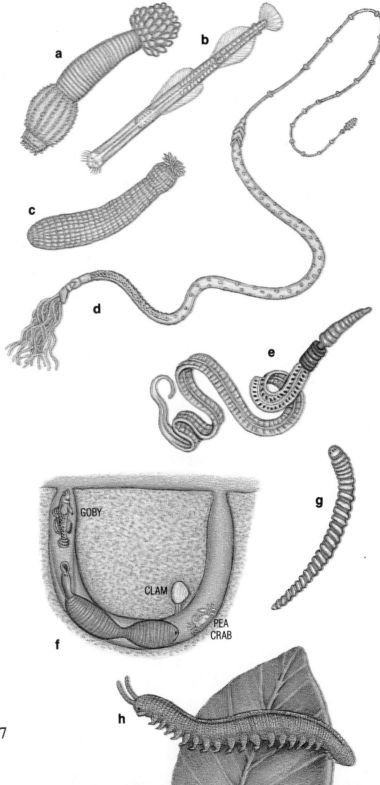

a

b

c

d

e

GOBY

CLAM

PEA CRAB

f

g

h

Arthropods

MORE THAN ONE MILLION species of animals all belong to the same group. It is the largest group in the animal world, called the arthropods. Although arthropods have no bones, they all have tubelike legs that bend.

Insects are arthropods with six legs. There are about a million known insect species (pages 30–41), including all ants, butterflies, beetles, and bees.

Spiders and scorpions are eight-legged arthropods. They are described with other arthropods called arachnids on page 42.

Arthropods with 10 legs, such as lobsters, are called crustaceans. The more than 45,000 species of crustaceans include crabs and shrimps (page 44).

Finally, centipedes and millipedes, which have many more than 10 legs, are illustrated on these two pages, along with some unusual arthropods.

Arthropods have hard crusts covering the outside of their bodies. This crust forms in pieces and is similar to the metal pieces of a knight's armor. Like armor, the pieces are connected in such a way that they can move. Where the pieces join together is called a joint. Most joints can bend. Arthropods use muscles inside the crust to bend their joints.

As arthropods grow, their bodies get too big for the crust covering them. Since the crust stretches very little and doesn't grow along with them, arthropods have to break out of the crust and make a new one. This process is called molting. During molting, the crust bursts and the arthropod crawls out of it. Freed of its old crust, the arthropod grows as a thick liquid oozes out of its body and slowly hardens into a new, larger crust. Until this new crust hardens, arthropods are in great danger because they are defenseless.

Most arthropods live on land. In addition to protecting their bodies, the crust helps arthropods keep water inside them so that they don't dry out.

Arthropods aren't the only animals with joints. Birds, mammals, and all the other animals with bones (pages 48–109) also have joints. In bony animals, a joint occurs where two bones meet. Without joints neither bony animals nor arthropods would be able to bend, twist, or turn their bodies as they do.

ARTHROPODS Insects, spiders, crabs, and the other animals pictured here are some of the more than one million species of arthropods. Arthropods have no bones, but they do have hard crusts covering their bodies. These crusts form in pieces. The places where one piece meets another are called joints. The word *arthropod* means "jointed leg."

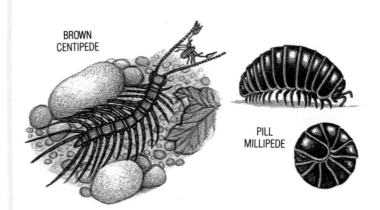

BROWN CENTIPEDE

PILL MILLIPEDE

During the day centipedes hide under leaves or stones. At night they creep along, using their large, poisonous claws to capture earthworms, slugs, and insects. There is one pair of legs on nearly every section of a centipede's body. When millipedes sense danger, they can curl up into a ball. If they have to, they give off a foul-smelling liquid to ward off an attacker. There are two pairs of legs on almost every section of a millipede's body.

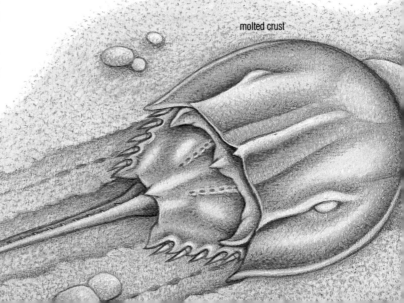

molted crust

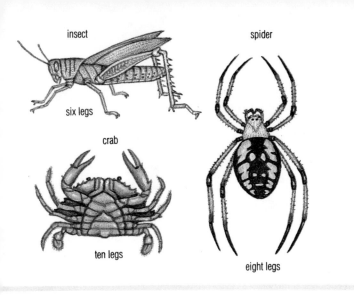

insect
six legs

spider
eight legs

crab
ten legs

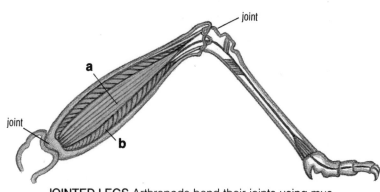

joint
joint
a
b

JOINTED LEGS Arthropods bend their joints using muscles attached from the inside. In this joint, one muscle (**a**) bends the leg; another muscle (**b**) straightens it out again.

Sea spiders live in the oceans, where they eat sponges, soft corals, and sea anemones.

A female symphyla attaches her sticky eggs to a moss plant.

This pauropod lives in soil among dead leaves.

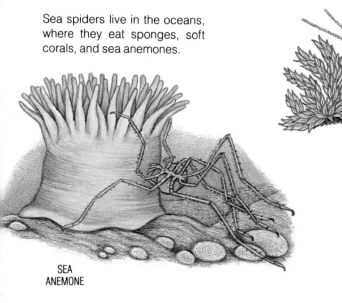

SEA ANEMONE

In shallow seas, horseshoe crabs crawl over the sand, breathing through gills. Using their leg pincers, they pick up mollusks and worms to eat. This horseshoe crab has molted (shed) the hard crust covering its body and grown a new one, which is starting to harden. Except for some turtles, few animals eat horseshoe crabs, but gulls eat many of the eggs that horseshoe crabs bury on the beach.

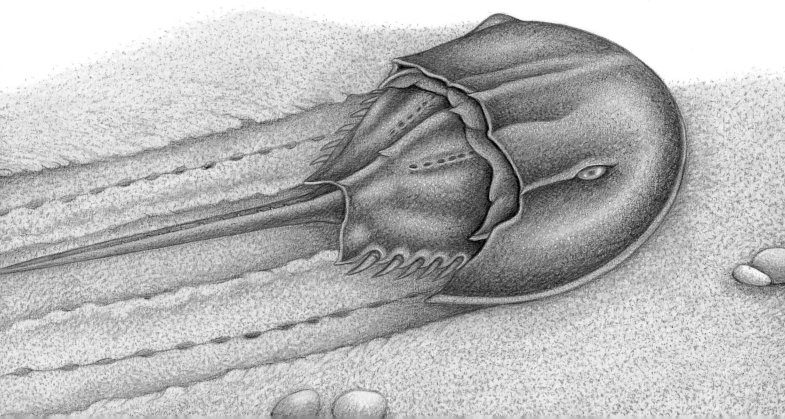

Insects

INSECTS FLY, RUN, swim, jump, tunnel, crawl, buzz, chirp, flash light, and even walk on water. They make silk, wax, paper, and honey. Some live where it is very hot, others where it is very cold. Still others live in caves, underground, in plants, or in fantastic homes they build.

For protection insects have poisonous stingers, sharp spines, and smelly liquids they shoot out at predators. Still, all over the world animals eat them. Even some plants eat them. But most plants need insects to help make new plants.

Some insects live together, ruled by a queen who lays 10,000 eggs a day. A few form armies or capture slaves. Altogether, insects have so many young each year that no one knows how many individual insects there really are.

Butterflies, bees, beetles, bugs, flies, ants, wasps, and grasshoppers are some of the million species of insects. With so many species, insects make up two thirds of all the animal species in the animal world. And all insects are arthropods.

The tough outer crusts on insect bodies are flexible and light and have a waxy coating. Like the crust itself, the wax helps prevent water from escaping out of an insect's body. Most insects live on land, where water can be hard to find, especially during dry weather.

The body of an adult insect is divided into three sections. The front section is the head, which contains the brain, eyes, mouthparts, and a pair of antennas, or feelers. Different insects use their antennas to taste, feel, or smell the world around them. The flexible antennas can pick up chemical signals sent by other insects, tell which way the wind is blowing, or find out how cold, hot, or damp the air is. As insects move, they can explore with their antennas.

Insects don't have noses, ears, or voice boxes. Just about all, though, have at least two eyes. Some have five. Insect eyes don't focus well, but they are able to detect movements around them. They also have their own way of seeing colors. To some, red looks black whereas green and orange both look yellow. Many insects can even see colors most other animals can't. Seeing these colors helps them find nectar and pollen in flowers.

INSECT MOUTHPARTS Insects use their special mouthparts for eating different kinds of food. Some insects bite and chew leaves. Others pierce the skin of large animals to feed on blood. Still others have long, hollow tubes that they use like straws to sip nectar from flowers.

mosquito

piercing parts

sipping parts

bee

chewing parts

butterfly

fly

beetle

chewing parts

spongy parts

INSECT LEGS Using their legs, insects can swim (a), jump (b), run (c), hold on tight (d), grasp (e), or dig (f).

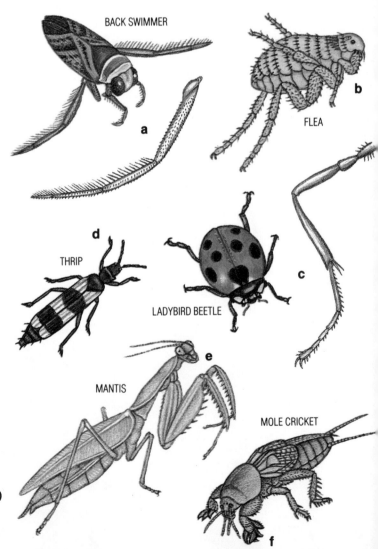

BACK SWIMMER

a

b

FLEA

d

c

THRIP

LADYBIRD BEETLE

e

MANTIS

MOLE CRICKET

f

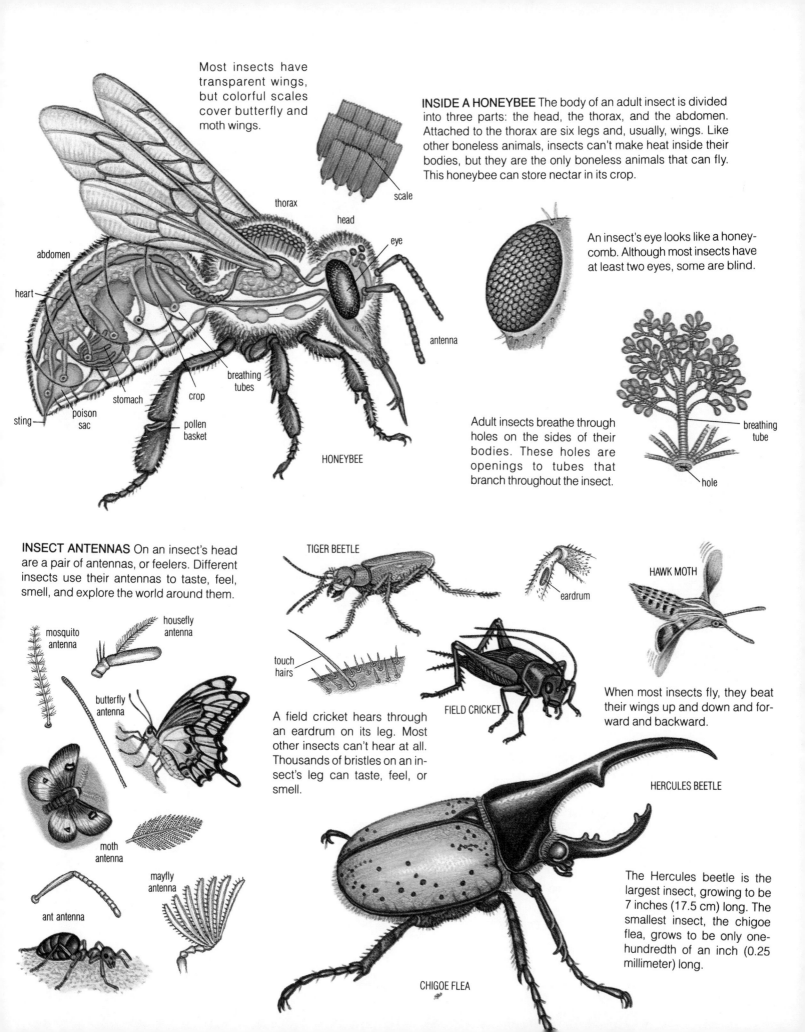

Most insects have transparent wings, but colorful scales cover butterfly and moth wings.

scale

thorax

head

eye

abdomen

heart

sting

poison sac

stomach

crop

pollen basket

breathing tubes

antenna

HONEYBEE

INSIDE A HONEYBEE The body of an adult insect is divided into three parts: the head, the thorax, and the abdomen. Attached to the thorax are six legs and, usually, wings. Like other boneless animals, insects can't make heat inside their bodies, but they are the only boneless animals that can fly. This honeybee can store nectar in its crop.

An insect's eye looks like a honeycomb. Although most insects have at least two eyes, some are blind.

Adult insects breathe through holes on the sides of their bodies. These holes are openings to tubes that branch throughout the insect.

breathing tube

hole

INSECT ANTENNAS On an insect's head are a pair of antennas, or feelers. Different insects use their antennas to taste, feel, smell, and explore the world around them.

mosquito antenna

housefly antenna

butterfly antenna

moth antenna

ant antenna

mayfly antenna

TIGER BEETLE

eardrum

touch hairs

FIELD CRICKET

A field cricket hears through an eardrum on its leg. Most other insects can't hear at all. Thousands of bristles on an insect's leg can taste, feel, or smell.

HAWK MOTH

When most insects fly, they beat their wings up and down and forward and backward.

HERCULES BEETLE

The Hercules beetle is the largest insect, growing to be 7 inches (17.5 cm) long. The smallest insect, the chigoe flea, grows to be only one-hundredth of an inch (0.25 millimeter) long.

CHIGOE FLEA

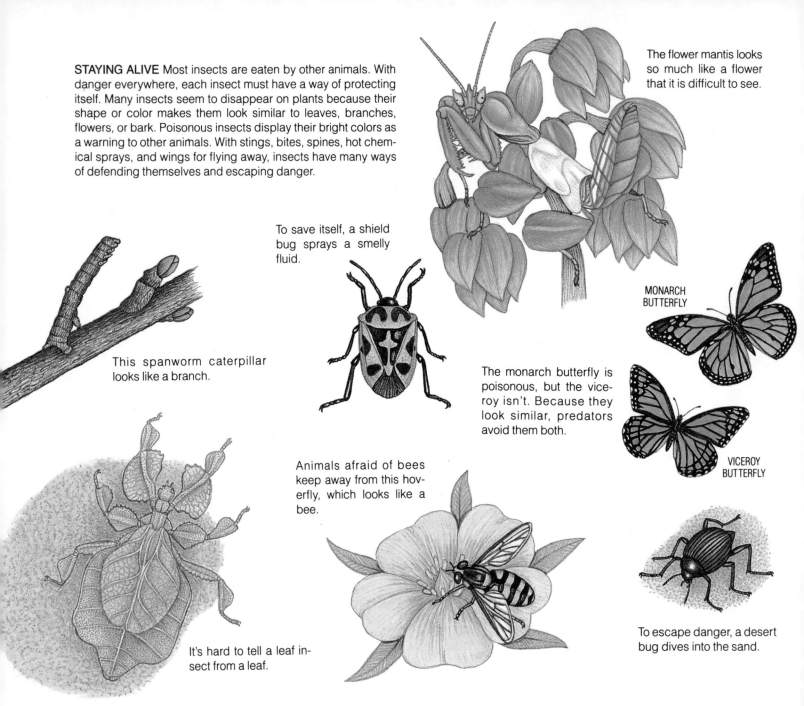

STAYING ALIVE Most insects are eaten by other animals. With danger everywhere, each insect must have a way of protecting itself. Many insects seem to disappear on plants because their shape or color makes them look similar to leaves, branches, flowers, or bark. Poisonous insects display their bright colors as a warning to other animals. With stings, bites, spines, hot chemical sprays, and wings for flying away, insects have many ways of defending themselves and escaping danger.

The flower mantis looks so much like a flower that it is difficult to see.

To save itself, a shield bug sprays a smelly fluid.

This spanworm caterpillar looks like a branch.

MONARCH BUTTERFLY

The monarch butterfly is poisonous, but the viceroy isn't. Because they look similar, predators avoid them both.

VICEROY BUTTERFLY

Animals afraid of bees keep away from this hoverfly, which looks like a bee.

It's hard to tell a leaf insect from a leaf.

To escape danger, a desert bug dives into the sand.

The middle section of an insect's body is the thorax, or chest. Attached to the thorax are legs and, in nearly all insects, wings. All adult insects have six legs. Besides using their legs for moving, insects use them to help clean their bodies. Sensitive bristles grow out of the legs. Different bristles can taste, feel, or smell. When a fly, for instance, lands on food, it can taste the food with its leg bristles before eating.

Inside an insect's tail section, or abdomen, are body parts for digesting food, getting rid of wastes, and reproducing.

Most insects can't hear, but grasshoppers, crickets, and a few others can. They have eardrums either on the sides of their abdomens or on their legs.

Insects have their own way of breathing. Instead of gills or lungs, nearly all adult insects have tiny air tubes (tracheal tubes) that branch throughout their bodies. Special openings all over an insect's body allow air into the tubes. When insects fly, their wing muscles help pump air in and out of their tubes.

Even though insects spend a lot of time on the ground, most can fly. By flying, they can move easily from place to place to find food, escape from danger, or discover safe spots to lay their eggs.

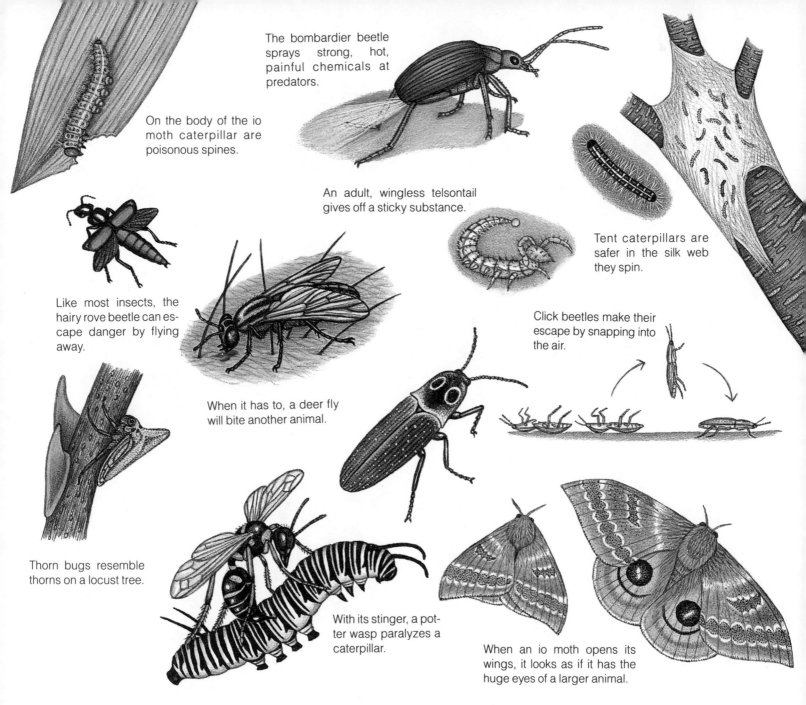

The bombardier beetle sprays strong, hot, painful chemicals at predators.

On the body of the io moth caterpillar are poisonous spines.

An adult, wingless telsontail gives off a sticky substance.

Tent caterpillars are safer in the silk web they spin.

Like most insects, the hairy rove beetle can escape danger by flying away.

Click beetles make their escape by snapping into the air.

When it has to, a deer fly will bite another animal.

Thorn bugs resemble thorns on a locust tree.

With its stinger, a potter wasp paralyzes a caterpillar.

When an io moth opens its wings, it looks as if it has the huge eyes of a larger animal.

How Insects Fly

Flying insects use their muscles to work their wings. To fly, insects move their wings not only up and down but also forward and backward. This is different from the way birds or bats fly.

Most insects have two pairs of wings. In some insects, when the front pair goes up the rear pair beats down. In others the two pairs move together, sometimes because the front and rear wings are hooked to each other. Beetles use only one pair of their wings for flying. The other pair serve as shields to protect their delicate flight wings. Instead of four wings, flies and mosquitoes have only two. In place of the other pair are two knobs that beat to help these insects steer.

Slow-flying butterflies beat their wings only 30 times a second. A housefly can beat its wings 200 times a second, and some gnats can beat theirs 1,000 times a second. Insects depend on their eyes and antennas to help them steer. They use the position of the sun or objects such as trees and rocks to help them find their way.

When insects hatch from their eggs, they are wingless. Some slowly grow wings as they get older. Others, such as butterflies and moths, spend the first part

FOOD FOR INSECTS Insects eat leaves, seeds, bark, wood, animal wastes, blood, skin, feathers, fur, hair, nectar, spiders, other insects, and other animals.

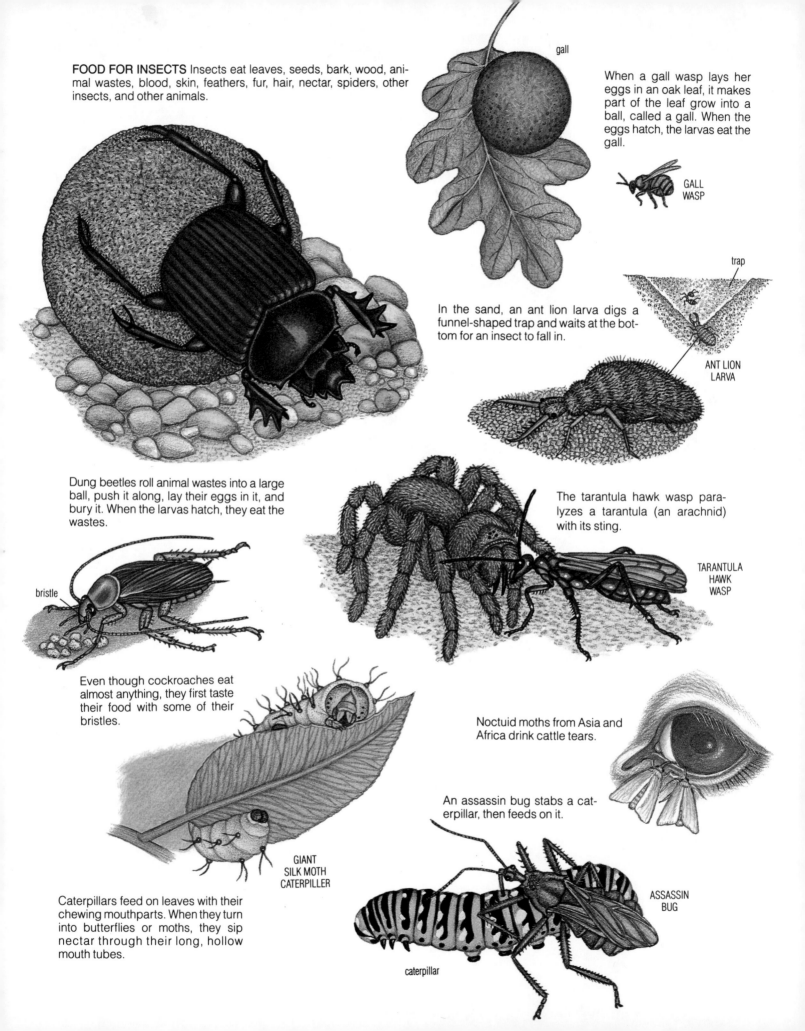

gall

When a gall wasp lays her eggs in an oak leaf, it makes part of the leaf grow into a ball, called a gall. When the eggs hatch, the larvas eat the gall.

GALL WASP

trap

In the sand, an ant lion larva digs a funnel-shaped trap and waits at the bottom for an insect to fall in.

ANT LION LARVA

Dung beetles roll animal wastes into a large ball, push it along, lay their eggs in it, and bury it. When the larvas hatch, they eat the wastes.

The tarantula hawk wasp paralyzes a tarantula (an arachnid) with its sting.

TARANTULA HAWK WASP

bristle

Even though cockroaches eat almost anything, they first taste their food with some of their bristles.

Noctuid moths from Asia and Africa drink cattle tears.

An assassin bug stabs a caterpillar, then feeds on it.

GIANT SILK MOTH CATERPILLER

ASSASSIN BUG

Caterpillars feed on leaves with their chewing mouthparts. When they turn into butterflies or moths, they sip nectar through their long, hollow mouth tubes.

caterpillar

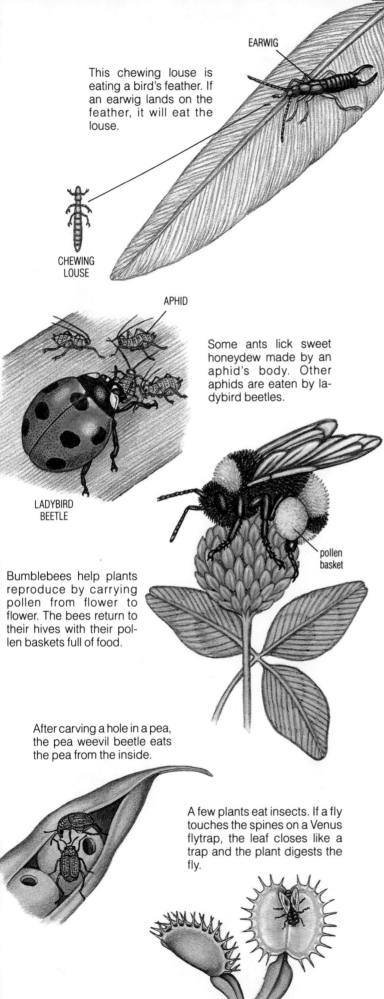

EARWIG

This chewing louse is eating a bird's feather. If an earwig lands on the feather, it will eat the louse.

CHEWING LOUSE

APHID

Some ants lick sweet honeydew made by an aphid's body. Other aphids are eaten by ladybird beetles.

LADYBIRD BEETLE

Bumblebees help plants reproduce by carrying pollen from flower to flower. The bees return to their hives with their pollen baskets full of food.

pollen basket

After carving a hole in a pea, the pea weevil beetle eats the pea from the inside.

A few plants eat insects. If a fly touches the spines on a Venus flytrap, the leaf closes like a trap and the plant digests the fly.

of their lives as wingless larvas called caterpillars. Only when they change into adults (pages 36–37) do they grow wings. Most insect wings are transparent, but butterfly and moth wings are covered by shiny or colorful scales.

Before flying, insects need to warm up their muscles. Since they can't generate heat inside their bodies, insects have to get it from the sun. Often, on cold days, some insects shiver to warm up.

Getting Food

As long as insects have enough sugar for energy to keep their muscles working, they can fly for hours. When they need more energy, they have to find food. Insects use their special mouthparts to eat different kinds of food (page 30). A grasshopper's mouthparts let it bite and chew leaves. Aphids bore into plant stems to steal plant juices. Many moths have a long, hollow tube, called a proboscis, which they use like a straw to sip sugary nectar from flowers. Mosquitoes pierce an animal's skin and drink blood, and lice eat feathers, fur, or the skin of the large animals on which they live. Some beetles eat wastes they find on the ground, some wasps kill other insects for food, and cockroaches eat just about anything.

Caterpillars have chewing mouthparts for eating plant leaves. But when they change into butterflies, their mouthparts change too. Butterflies flit from flower to flower sipping nectar.

Different kinds of insects eat seeds, leaves, wood, fruit, sap, or nectar. If too many insects eat the same plant, they can destroy it. This rarely happens. In fact, each year insects help many species of plants reproduce. They do this by carrying pollen from one flower to another of the same species.

Pollen is picked up when insects land on flowers. Insects are lured to flowers by their dazzling colors and delicious scents. Honeybees, for example, fly from flower to flower in search of sweet nectar and protein-rich pollen. As they move around on the flowers, their bodies rub against the flower parts and some pollen sticks to them. When they fly to another flower of the same species, some of the pollen rubs off their bodies. If this pollen reaches female flower parts, the flower can make new seeds. Every year, billions of butterflies, moths, and bees carry pollen from flower to flower.

35

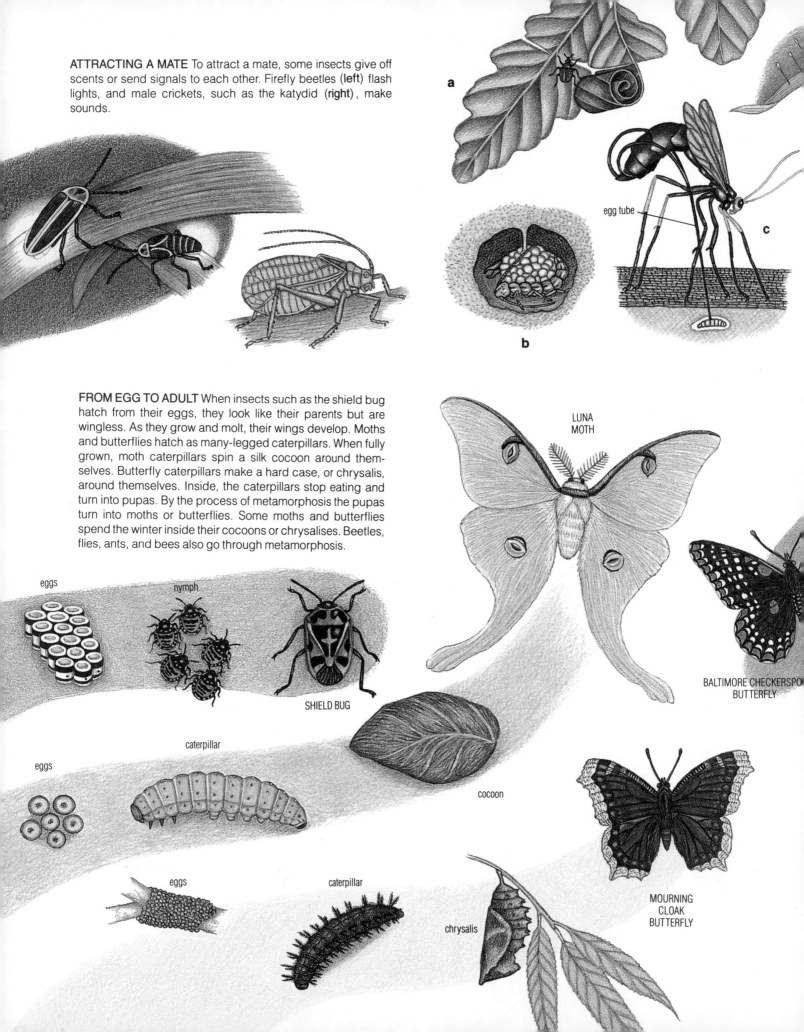

ATTRACTING A MATE To attract a mate, some insects give off scents or send signals to each other. Firefly beetles (**left**) flash lights, and male crickets, such as the katydid (**right**), make sounds.

a

egg tube

c

b

FROM EGG TO ADULT When insects such as the shield bug hatch from their eggs, they look like their parents but are wingless. As they grow and molt, their wings develop. Moths and butterflies hatch as many-legged caterpillars. When fully grown, moth caterpillars spin a silk cocoon around themselves. Butterfly caterpillars make a hard case, or chrysalis, around themselves. Inside, the caterpillars stop eating and turn into pupas. By the process of metamorphosis the pupas turn into moths or butterflies. Some moths and butterflies spend the winter inside their cocoons or chrysalises. Beetles, flies, ants, and bees also go through metamorphosis.

LUNA MOTH

eggs

nymph

SHIELD BUG

BALTIMORE CHECKERSPO
BUTTERFLY

eggs

caterpillar

cocoon

eggs

caterpillar

chrysalis

MOURNING
CLOAK
BUTTERFLY

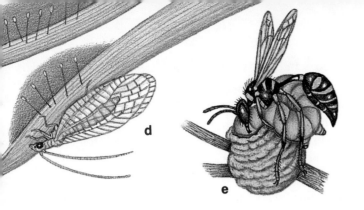

LAYING EGGS Female insects lay batches of their eggs in safe places, making it difficult for predators to find them all. A leaf roller beetle (**a**) rolls her eggs inside a leaf. Unlike most insects, the japyx (**b**) guards her eggs. The ichneumon wasp (**c**) sticks her long egg tube under tree bark and lays her eggs on top of a hidden caterpillar. When her young hatch, they eat the caterpillar. Lacewings (**d**) lay their eggs on leaves. The potter wasp (**e**) builds a nest of clay for her eggs.

YELLOW
SWALLOWTAIL
BUTTERFLY

COMMON
BLUE
BUTTERFLY

ATLAS
MOTH

After honeybees find flowers rich in nectar and pollen, they fly back to their hives and start dancing in front of other bees. From these dances, the other bees can figure out where they have to fly to find the same flowers the dancers just visited. Dancing is just one of the remarkable ways in which insects communicate with one another. Grasshoppers and crickets make sounds by rubbing together parts of their bodies. Ants touch antennas, moths give off scents that travel for miles, and firefly beetles flash light signals to one another. Some insects send signals that identify their species to other insects. With a million insect species, each insect must locate a mate belonging to its own species. But insects also communicate with other animals. Many poisonous insects show off their bright colors to warn other animals to stay away.

From Egg to Insect

When nearly all insects mate, the male releases his sperm inside the female's body. When she is ready to lay her eggs, the female takes great care to find places where her eggs will not dry out and where they will be safe from other animals or cold weather. Some females hide their eggs under tree bark, on leaves, underwater, or on the bodies of other animals. Others poke holes in the ground or in plant stems, then lay their eggs inside. Often, insects lay their eggs on certain plants and animals that their babies can eat after hatching.

Insects lay lots of eggs. Although many of these eggs do hatch, most of the babies die or are eaten before they can mature and lay eggs of their own. Most insects don't take care of their eggs; in fact, they die soon after laying the eggs. However, all ants and termites and some bees and wasps not only care for their eggs but also help raise their young (page 40).

At hatching, many kinds of insects resemble their parents except that they are tiny and wingless. As they grow, they molt several times and their wings develop gradually. When they reach adult size, molting stops.

Moths, butterflies, bees, flies, beetles, and other insects don't look like their parents on hatching from their eggs. During their lives they undergo an incredible change, called metamorphosis, which makes them look like their parents.

Butterflies and moths start life as many-legged caterpillars. As soon as they hatch from their eggs, they

37

start chewing leaves and growing. The faster they grow, the more often they have to molt. When they are fully grown, they stop eating, spin a silk thread, and hang from it. Silk is produced by special glands near their mouths.

Moth caterpillars continue to spin silk all around the outside of their bodies, forming a cocoon. Butterfly caterpillars give off a substance that hardens around them into a case called a chrysalis. Inside its cocoon or chrysalis, a caterpillar doesn't eat or move. Its body changes completely: it grows wings, changes mouth-parts, and winds up with only six legs, like all adult insects. When the change is complete, the cocoon or chrysalis splits open and the moth or butterfly pulls itself out. After pumping blood into its wings, the moth or butterfly waits for its wings to dry, then flies off to sip nectar and mate.

Where winter months are cold, some butterflies migrate thousands of miles each year to places where the weather will be warm during those months. Other insects stay where they are and hibernate through winter, hidden under tree bark or in the soil.

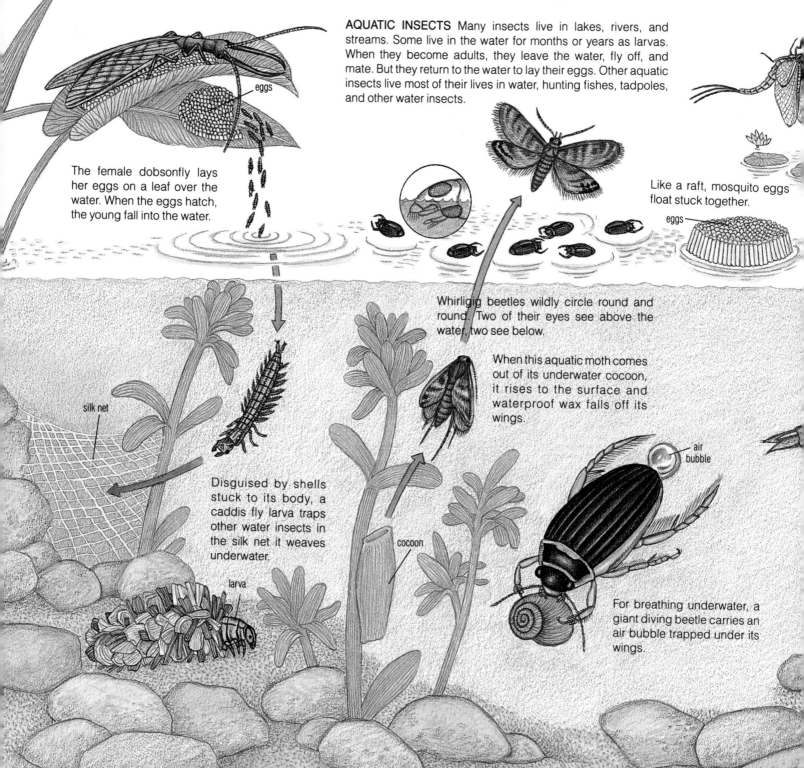

AQUATIC INSECTS Many insects live in lakes, rivers, and streams. Some live in the water for months or years as larvas. When they become adults, they leave the water, fly off, and mate. But they return to the water to lay their eggs. Other aquatic insects live most of their lives in water, hunting fishes, tadpoles, and other water insects.

eggs

The female dobsonfly lays her eggs on a leaf over the water. When the eggs hatch, the young fall into the water.

Like a raft, mosquito eggs float stuck together.

eggs

Whirligig beetles wildly circle round and round. Two of their eyes see above the water, two see below.

When this aquatic moth comes out of its underwater cocoon, it rises to the surface and waterproof wax falls off its wings.

silk net

Disguised by shells stuck to its body, a caddis fly larva traps other water insects in the silk net it weaves underwater.

cocoon

larva

air bubble

For breathing underwater, a giant diving beetle carries an air bubble trapped under its wings.

Water Insects

Only a very few insects live in the oceans, but many live part of their lives in lakes, ponds, and rivers. Some of these water insects live underwater for years as larvas or nymphs (page 36), breathing through gills. With their pincerlike mouthparts they capture tadpoles, small fishes, and other aquatic insects. Like all arthropods, they molt many times.

When water insects are ready to change into adults, they leave the water and molt one more time. As a result of this molt, they have wings and can fly off in search of a mate. After mating, females return to the water to lay their eggs.

Other aquatic insects don't breathe through gills. Some have special tubes that stick out of the water into the air. Others capture air bubbles under their wings for breathing a short time underwater. Many of these water insects spend their entire lives swimming in the water.

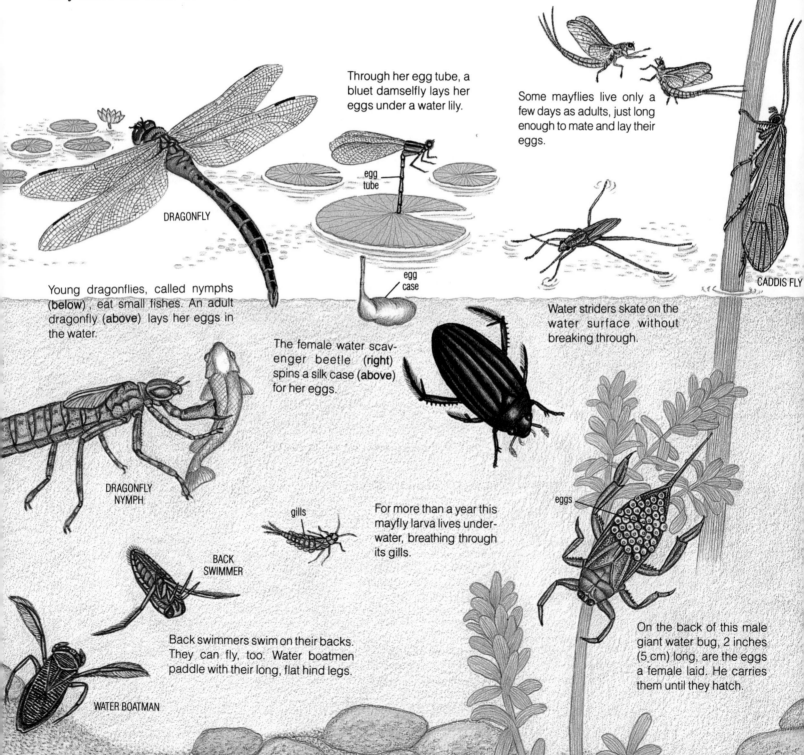

Through her egg tube, a bluet damselfly lays her eggs under a water lily.

Some mayflies live only a few days as adults, just long enough to mate and lay their eggs.

DRAGONFLY

egg tube

egg case

CADDIS FLY

Young dragonflies, called nymphs (**below**), eat small fishes. An adult dragonfly (**above**) lays her eggs in the water.

The female water scavenger beetle (**right**) spins a silk case (**above**) for her eggs.

Water striders skate on the water surface without breaking through.

DRAGONFLY NYMPH

gills

For more than a year this mayfly larva lives underwater, breathing through its gills.

eggs

BACK SWIMMER

Back swimmers swim on their backs. They can fly, too. Water boatmen paddle with their long, flat hind legs.

WATER BOATMAN

On the back of this male giant water bug, 2 inches (5 cm) long, are the eggs a female laid. He carries them until they hatch.

Social Insects

Except when they mate, many insects spend their lives alone. But ants, termites, and some species of bees and wasps live in groups or societies. Each kind of insect society builds a nest, which is ruled by a queen. The queen's job is to lay eggs. Most of her eggs hatch into future workers. Every worker has a job to do too. Some build, clean, take care of the young, find food, or guard their nest. No member of the colony can live alone. Each needs the others to stay alive; they all belong to one family.

Social insects are expert builders. Their spectacular homes bustle with activity as hundreds of thousands of workers make sure that the daily needs of the queen and her family are met. In the animal world, no other groups of animals live and work together the way the social insects do.

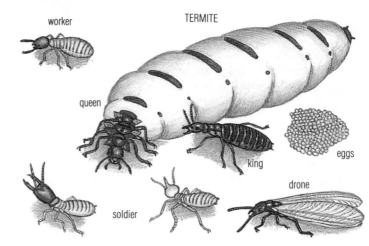

TERMITES Some termites can build nests 20 feet (6 m) high, which have chambers and tunnels inside. The termite queen and king live in the largest chamber. The queen can lay 10,000 eggs a day. From the eggs develop blind, wingless workers and soldiers. Hundreds of thousands of termites can live in one nest, all of them brothers and sisters.

Worker termites lick the queen to clean her, care for the eggs and young, and feed the queen and king. Workers build shafts so that air can flow in and out of the nest. They also dig underground tunnels to get food. Most termites eat wood, dead leaves, or dry grass. To defend the nest, some soldier termites spray a sticky, poisonous liquid on insects, such as ants, that attack them.

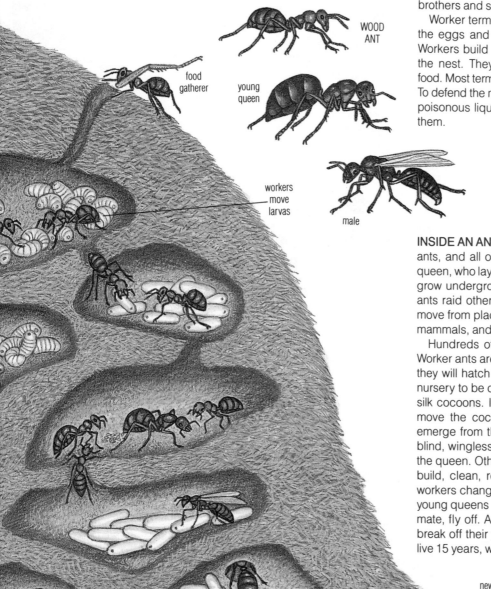

INSIDE AN ANT COLONY There are more than 10,000 species of ants, and all of them live in colonies. Each colony is ruled by a queen, who lays eggs. Some ant colonies collect and store seeds, grow underground gardens, or weave leaves together. Amazon ants raid other ant colonies and capture slaves. And army ants move from place to place devouring snakes, nesting birds, small mammals, and any other animals that get in their way.

Hundreds of thousands of ants live in this wood ant colony. Worker ants are carrying the queen's eggs into a chamber, where they will hatch into helpless larvas. The larvas are moved into a nursery to be cared for and fed. Like moths, most ant larvas spin silk cocoons. Inside the cocoons they become pupas. Workers move the cocoons to another chamber. Eventually adult ants emerge from the cocoons. Most of the queen's eggs hatch into blind, wingless female workers. Some workers feed and care for the queen. Others gather food, care for the larvas and pupas, or build, clean, repair, or defend the nest. Every few months the workers change jobs. At certain times, some pupas develop into young queens and males. Both grow wings and, when it is time to mate, fly off. After mating, the males die. The new queens land, break off their wings, and start their own colonies. A queen may live 15 years, whereas workers live five or six.

PAPER WASP

worker egg

worker

honey cell

fanner

repairer

food storer

pollen cell

cleaner

queen

larva

egg

drone

worker

dancing scout

wax maker

wax cell

queen cell

HONEYBEE

food scout

guard

pollen collector

SOCIAL WASPS Many wasps live alone, but not the paper wasp. To make her nest, a queen paper wasp chews wood. When she spits it out, it dries into paper. She shapes the paper into a few six-sided cells. Into each cell she lays an egg. The eggs hatch into female larvas, which are fed chewed-up insects and spiders by the queen. When the larvas develop into workers, they build more cells for more eggs. While the queen lays eggs, the workers take care of the nest and the new wasps. Towards autumn, drones, or male wasps, develop. They fly off to mate with young queens. Only the mated young queens live. All the other wasps in the nest die. During winter a young queen hibernates in a safe place. In spring she starts her own nest.

INSIDE A HIVE Each honeybee in this hive has a job to do. The large queen bee is busy laying eggs while workers feed, clean, and protect her. Other workers place each egg into its own six-sided cell made of beeswax. The eggs hatch into larvas, which are fed until they change into adults. Most of the bees in the hive are workers, and all workers are females. Some workers are nurses, which care for and feed the young. Others are wax makers, cleaners, repairers, food storers, cell builders, pollen collectors, food scouts, and guards. Guards are ready to sting any animal or person that gets too close to the hive. When a food scout returns to the hive, she does a dance that tells the other bees where to fly to find food. Honeybees carry pollen back to the hive and store it in pollen cells. They also carry nectar back in their crop, cough it up, and store it in honey cells. Other worker bees fan the nectar by beating their wings, and slowly it turns into honey. Male bees are called drones. In the hive there are only a few dozen drones. When the hive becomes overcrowded, a new queen hatches. The old queen flies off with a swarm of workers to start a new hive. The new queen flies off with the drones and mates with a few of them. Then the drones die. The new queen returns to the hive and takes over the task of laying eggs.

41

Arachnids

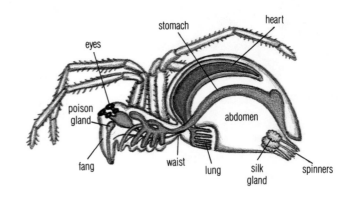

SPIDERS, SCORPIONS, ticks, and mites may look like insects, but they aren't. They have eight legs, not six. They don't have antennas or wings as insects do, and their bodies are divided into two main sections, not three. But they are all arthropods, and they all belong to the same group, called arachnids.

All spiders can spin silk. Silk is a liquid protein that hardens when it touches air. Spiders produce silk from special glands. The silk comes out of silk spinners at the rear of their bodies.

A spider can make more than one kind of silk. Some silk threads are sticky, others are not. Claws on the tips of a spider's legs make it easy for the spider to handle its silk. Spiders use their silk to make cases for their eggs, to build nests for their young, to line their tunnels, or to spin sticky webs to trap insects.

Web-spinning spiders hatch from their eggs knowing how to spin their complicated webs. Each kind of spider builds its own kind of web. When an insect is caught in a web, the web shakes, letting a spider know there may be food to eat. As soon as a spider finds the trapped insect, it wraps the insect in silk threads and bites it with poisonous fangs. The poison paralyzes the helpless insect and turns the insect's insides into a liquid. When the spider gets hungry, it pierces the insect and drinks in as much of the liquid as it needs. The rest is left for later. Should its web get damaged, a spider spins more silk to repair any holes.

Not all spiders make webs. Some live in homes they dig in the ground. When they need food, they come out to hunt, pouncing on insects and biting them with their poisonous fangs.

A few spiders live underwater in silk webs. Like all spiders, they need to breathe air into their lungs. So they fill their webs with air bubbles that they carry down with them from the surface.

More than half of the 75,000 species of arachnids are spiders. Most of the rest are very small mites and ticks. Many mites and ticks live on the bodies of large animals and plants, often causing diseases. Others hunt roundworms in the soil or eat insect eggs.

INSIDE A SPIDER Spiders aren't insects; they are arachnids, with eight legs. Their bodies are divided into two main sections connected at a narrow waist. Most spiders have eight simple eyes, and almost all have poisonous fangs. Spiders produce silk from silk glands. Many, but not all, use their silk to spin webs.

ARACHNIDS Spiders, scorpions, mites, ticks, and harvestmen make up the group of arthropods called arachnids.

There are more than 20,000 species of very small mites and ticks. Many live on animals, irritating them by eating their feathers, fur, or blood. Others eat insect eggs.

Daddy longlegs are harvestmen. Nearly all wave their second pair of legs when disturbed.

Although the false scorpion has no stinger, it uses the poison in its pincer to capture insects.

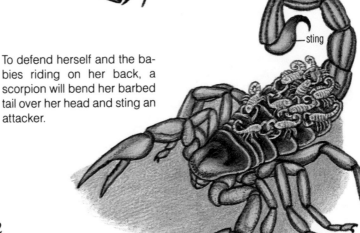

To defend herself and the babies riding on her back, a scorpion will bend her barbed tail over her head and sting an attacker.

42

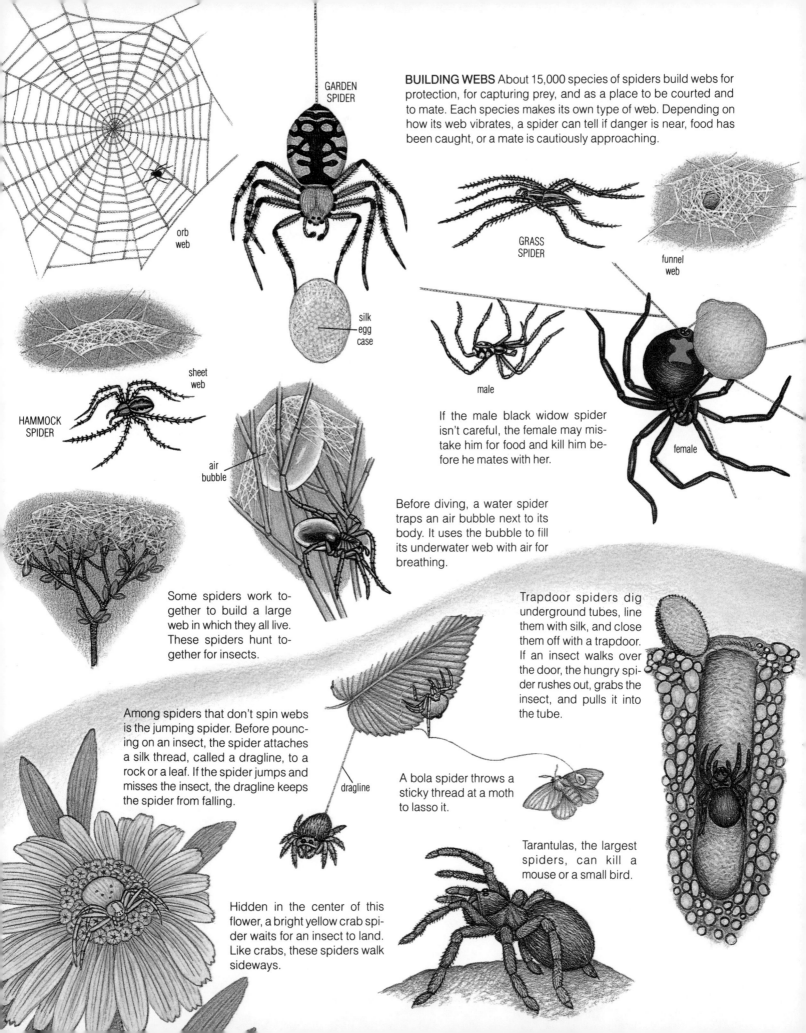

orb web

GARDEN SPIDER

BUILDING WEBS About 15,000 species of spiders build webs for protection, for capturing prey, and as a place to be courted and to mate. Each species makes its own type of web. Depending on how its web vibrates, a spider can tell if danger is near, food has been caught, or a mate is cautiously approaching.

GRASS SPIDER

funnel web

silk egg case

sheet web

HAMMOCK SPIDER

air bubble

male

If the male black widow spider isn't careful, the female may mistake him for food and kill him before he mates with her.

female

Before diving, a water spider traps an air bubble next to its body. It uses the bubble to fill its underwater web with air for breathing.

Some spiders work together to build a large web in which they all live. These spiders hunt together for insects.

Trapdoor spiders dig underground tubes, line them with silk, and close them off with a trapdoor. If an insect walks over the door, the hungry spider rushes out, grabs the insect, and pulls it into the tube.

Among spiders that don't spin webs is the jumping spider. Before pouncing on an insect, the spider attaches a silk thread, called a dragline, to a rock or a leaf. If the spider jumps and misses the insect, the dragline keeps the spider from falling.

dragline

A bola spider throws a sticky thread at a moth to lasso it.

Hidden in the center of this flower, a bright yellow crab spider waits for an insect to land. Like crabs, these spiders walk sideways.

Tarantulas, the largest spiders, can kill a mouse or a small bird.

Crustaceans

INSIDE A CRAYFISH Crayfishes belong to the group of arthropods called crustaceans. They have two pairs of head antennas, gills for breathing underwater, and five pairs of legs. At the end of the first pair of legs are large claws. The crust covering the crayfish forms a thick, hard, colored shield, or carapace. Until the female crayfish's eggs hatch, she carries them attached to her body.

S TEP BY STEP, a crab slowly crawls sideways on its spindly legs across the sea floor. Crabs belong to the group of arthropods called crustaceans. Lobsters, shrimps, crayfishes, barnacles, and water fleas are some of the more than 45,000 crustacean species.

Unlike other arthropods, nearly all crustaceans live underwater. Only a few, such as wood lice, live their entire lives on land. The smallest crustaceans are tiny water fleas that grow only one hundredth of an inch (0.25 mm) long. The largest crabs, though, can grow 2.5 feet (75 cm) long and have a leg span of 9 feet (2.7 m).

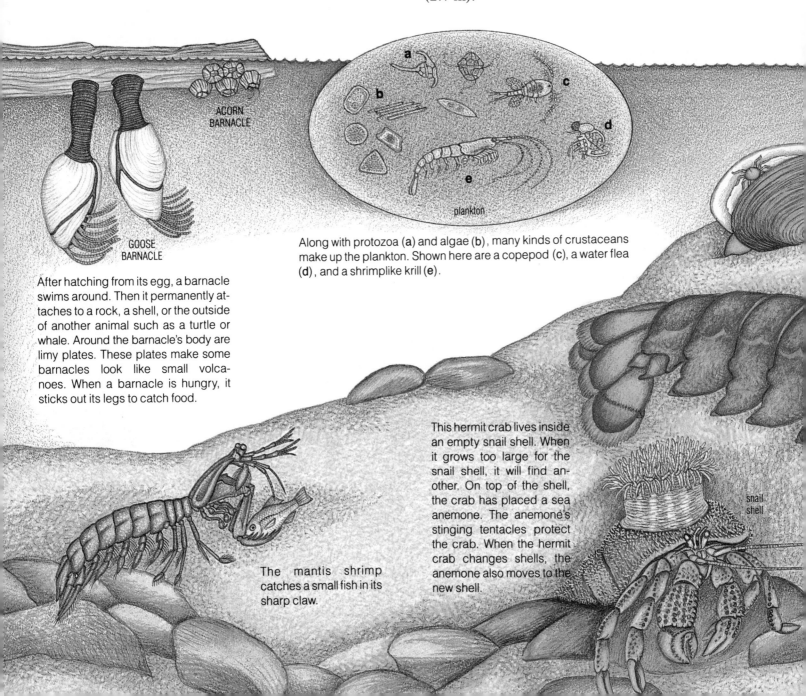

Along with protozoa (**a**) and algae (**b**), many kinds of crustaceans make up the plankton. Shown here are a copepod (**c**), a water flea (**d**), and a shrimplike krill (**e**).

After hatching from its egg, a barnacle swims around. Then it permanently attaches to a rock, a shell, or the outside of another animal such as a turtle or whale. Around the barnacle's body are limy plates. These plates make some barnacles look like small volcanoes. When a barnacle is hungry, it sticks out its legs to catch food.

The mantis shrimp catches a small fish in its sharp claw.

This hermit crab lives inside an empty snail shell. When it grows too large for the snail shell, it will find another. On top of the shell, the crab has placed a sea anemone. The anemone's stinging tentacles protect the crab. When the hermit crab changes shells, the anemone also moves to the new shell.

snail shell

Crustaceans have some body parts that other adult arthropods lack. Almost all crustaceans have two pairs of antennas on their heads, not one. Some have eyes on movable stalks. Most have gills for breathing underwater. And many female crustaceans have flaps or pouches for carrying around their unhatched eggs.

Like all arthropods, crustaceans have an outer crust on their bodies. In many large crustaceans, such as crabs and lobsters, part of this crust forms a thick, colored, extra-hard, one-piece shield, called a carapace. The carapace offers extra protection for the delicate, boneless body under it.

Crustaceans have at least five pairs of legs. On lobsters, crabs, and crayfishes the first pair of legs end in claws. These pincer claws are used to catch and crush food, to hold on to seaweed, and to move small rocks or shells. They also serve as powerful weapons against attack by hungry fishes and octopuses.

Near the ocean surface live many tiny crustaceans such as copepods, shrimplike krill, and some water fleas. Their vast numbers make up an important part of the plankton. Copepods and krill are a favorite food of many fishes, basking sharks, seals, and toothless whales (page 94).

Some adult crabs leave the water to live on the seashore, in sand dunes, or even in forests. During the day most hide under stones or in burrows they dig. At night they prowl, hunting for food. When it is time to reproduce, female land crabs return with their eggs to the sea so that their young can grow up in the water.

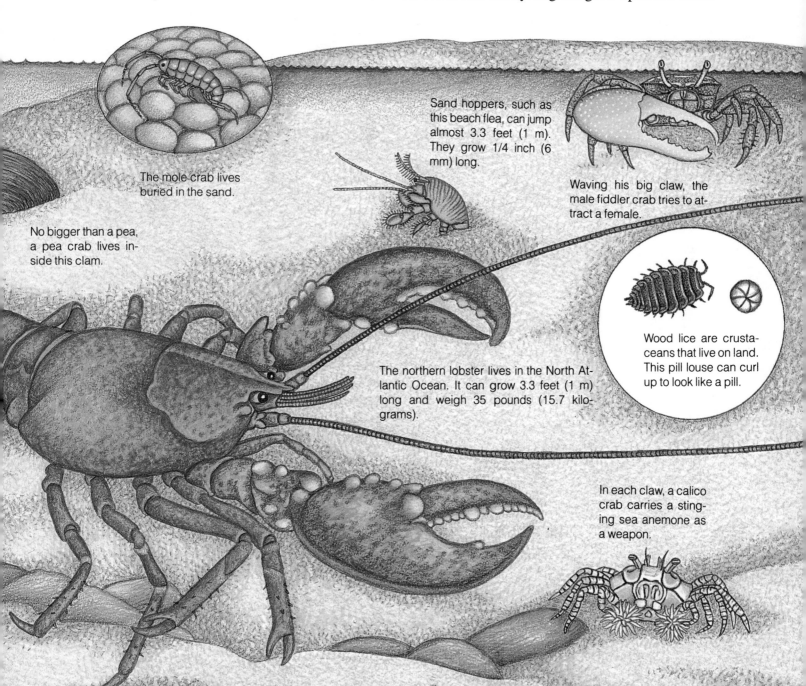

The mole crab lives buried in the sand.

No bigger than a pea, a pea crab lives inside this clam.

Sand hoppers, such as this beach flea, can jump almost 3.3 feet (1 m). They grow 1/4 inch (6 mm) long.

Waving his big claw, the male fiddler crab tries to attract a female.

The northern lobster lives in the North Atlantic Ocean. It can grow 3.3 feet (1 m) long and weigh 35 pounds (15.7 kilograms).

Wood lice are crustaceans that live on land. This pill louse can curl up to look like a pill.

In each claw, a calico crab carries a stinging sea anemone as a weapon.

INSIDE A SEA STAR This sea star has five arms extending from the center of its body. Under each arm are rows of tiny, hollow tube feet. The tube feet are connected to canals that run throughout the sea star's body. Tiny suction cups at the ends of the tube feet grip tightly to slippery rocks and shells. Just under the sea star's skin are limy plates. From these plates, spines push out through the skin. Also sticking out of the skin are tiny, fingerlike gills. Special pincers on top keep these delicate gills clean by picking off sand and dust. Like all echinoderms, or spiny-skinned animals, sea stars live in the sea and can't survive very long out of water.

stomach

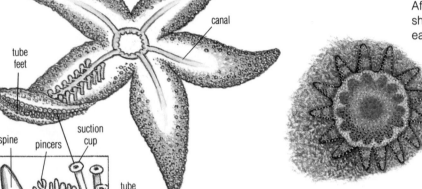

canal

tube
feet

spine   pincers   suction
cup

tube
foot

gills

After much hard work, a Forbes sea star pulls open an oyster's shells just slightly, sticks its stomach between the shells, and eats the oyster.

If a blue Pacific sea star (**right**) loses an arm, it grows a new one. The broken arm grows a complete body around itself. The spiny sun star (**left**) has 14 arms.

arm

Spiny-Skinned Animals

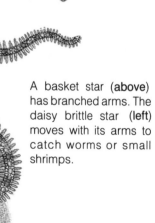

A basket star (**above**) has branched arms. The daisy brittle star (**left**) moves with its arms to catch worms or small shrimps.

I N THE SHALLOW ocean waters where it lives, a sea star senses an oyster nearby. Slowly, it moves its five-pointed body toward the oyster. One of its five arms leads the way for the others. On the underside of each arm are rows of tiny hollow tube feet.

When it reaches the oyster, the sea star spreads its five arms over the oyster's two shells. Suction cups at the ends of the tube feet clamp tightly to the shells. Using its muscles, the hungry sea star tries to pull the shells apart. After a while the oyster's shells open slightly. The sea star turns its stomach inside out and slides it out of its mouth into the opening. Once inside the oyster, the sea star's stomach pours juices over the soft oyster body. When the oyster has turned into a liquid, the sea star's stomach soaks it up. Then the sea star pulls its stomach back into its body.

Sea stars are spiny-skinned animals, or echino-

46

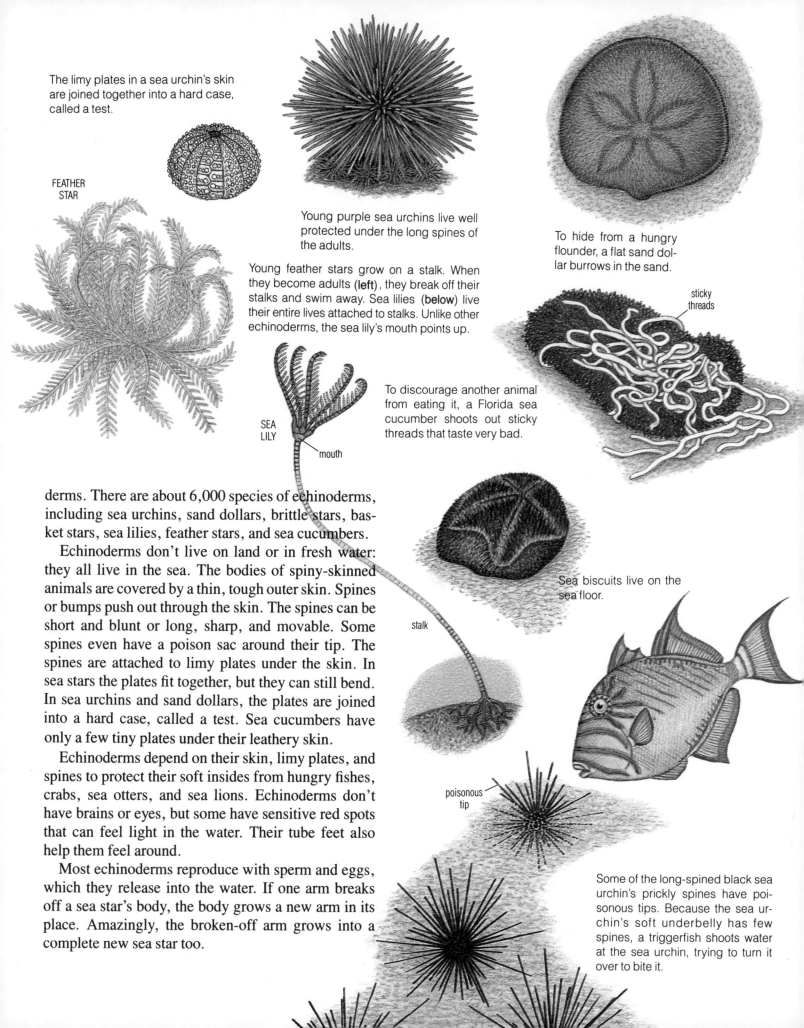

The limy plates in a sea urchin's skin are joined together into a hard case, called a test.

FEATHER STAR

Young purple sea urchins live well protected under the long spines of the adults.

Young feather stars grow on a stalk. When they become adults (**left**), they break off their stalks and swim away. Sea lilies (**below**) live their entire lives attached to stalks. Unlike other echinoderms, the sea lily's mouth points up.

SEA LILY

mouth

stalk

To hide from a hungry flounder, a flat sand dollar burrows in the sand.

sticky threads

To discourage another animal from eating it, a Florida sea cucumber shoots out sticky threads that taste very bad.

Sea biscuits live on the sea floor.

poisonous tip

derms. There are about 6,000 species of echinoderms, including sea urchins, sand dollars, brittle stars, basket stars, sea lilies, feather stars, and sea cucumbers.

Echinoderms don't live on land or in fresh water: they all live in the sea. The bodies of spiny-skinned animals are covered by a thin, tough outer skin. Spines or bumps push out through the skin. The spines can be short and blunt or long, sharp, and movable. Some spines even have a poison sac around their tip. The spines are attached to limy plates under the skin. In sea stars the plates fit together, but they can still bend. In sea urchins and sand dollars, the plates are joined into a hard case, called a test. Sea cucumbers have only a few tiny plates under their leathery skin.

Echinoderms depend on their skin, limy plates, and spines to protect their soft insides from hungry fishes, crabs, sea otters, and sea lions. Echinoderms don't have brains or eyes, but some have sensitive red spots that can feel light in the water. Their tube feet also help them feel around.

Most echinoderms reproduce with sperm and eggs, which they release into the water. If one arm breaks off a sea star's body, the body grows a new arm in its place. Amazingly, the broken-off arm grows into a complete new sea star too.

Some of the long-spined black sea urchin's prickly spines have poisonous tips. Because the sea urchin's soft underbelly has few spines, a triggerfish shoots water at the sea urchin, trying to turn it over to bite it.

Fishes

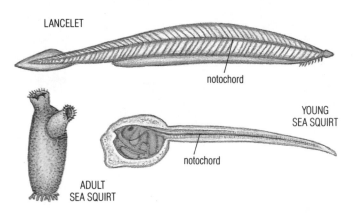

LANCELET

notochord

YOUNG
SEA SQUIRT

notochord

ADULT
SEA SQUIRT

IN THE CLEAR, sunlit waters of a coral reef; in the
near-total darkness of the deep seas; and even in
cool, rushing mountain streams live many, many fishes.

Fishes are the largest group of animals with bones.
Bones make up a fish's skeleton. They support the
fish's body and help give it shape. Bones also protect
delicate body parts such as nerves and the brain.

Running through a fish's body are bones called
vertebrae. All of the vertebrae make up the backbone.
Animals with backbones are called vertebrates.

In addition to fishes, amphibians (page 60), reptiles
(page 64), birds (page 70), and mammals (page 84)
are also vertebrates. There are only 43,000 species of
vertebrates. They include the fastest swimmers, the
most expert fliers, and the cleverest, the largest, and
the most intelligent animals. The rest of the animals in
this book are vertebrates.

Nearly all adult vertebrates have skeletons made of
strong, hard bone. Only some adult fishes, such as
sharks and rays, have skeletons made of cartilage.
Cartilage is softer, lighter, and more flexible than bone.

Attached to a fish's skeleton are sheets of muscles.
Bones can't move by themselves: muscles move them.
Most of a fish's weight comes from the very strong
muscles it uses for swimming.

Running down the center of the lancelet's body is an elastic rod
called a notochord. The notochord supports the body. Young
sea squirts also have a notochord. But when they become adults,
the notochord disappears. All animals that have a notochord
sometime during their lives are called chordates. Although a
lancelet and a sea squirt are shown here, neither is a fish.

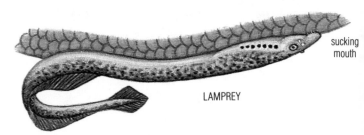

sucking
mouth

LAMPREY

Lampreys and hagfishes are jawless fishes. They live in salt
water and in fresh water. With its suction mouth, a lamprey
attaches itself to another fish. Then it drills into the fish's flesh
with its sharp teeth and sucks out the fish's blood. Hagfishes use
their rasping tongues to drill into a dead or dying fish. They eat
the insides, leaving behind just skin and bones. Only about 50
fish species have no jaws.

How Fishes Swim

Fishes are superb swimmers. When most fishes
swim, their muscles ripple from head to tail, bending
their bodies from side to side. Bending presses a fish's
body against the water and thrusts the fish forward.

A fish's tail works together with its fins to help push
the fish along, steer it, and keep it balanced. Top and
bottom fins help the fish move straight ahead. Side fins
keep the fish from tilting over. Each species of fish has
fins that are the right size and shape for its body. Fishes
such as marlins and sailfishes can fold down some of
their fins to swim at top speed. Other fishes, such as
rays, flap their broad fins up and down like wings.
Only a few fishes have no fins.

Swimming uses up a lot of energy. Turning, slowing
down, darting about, cruising, speeding up, stopping,
and avoiding other fishes are complicated movements.

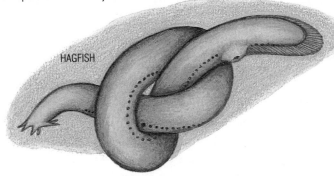

HAGFISH

As they swim, most fishes bend their
bodies from side to side. Fins help
fishes steer, turn, slow down, swim
smoothly, and keep from tilting. Torpedo-shaped fishes speed through
the water. Flat-bodied fishes live
close to the sea floor.

fin

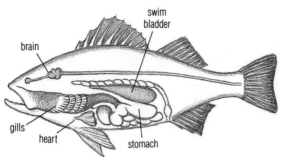

swim bladder

brain

gills

heart

stomach

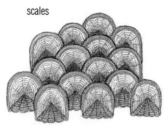

scales

FISHES Almost half of all species of bony animals are fishes. Some live in the oceans, others in rivers and lakes. Only a few species live part of their lives in salt water and part in fresh water. Most fishes are expert swimmers.

INSIDE A STRIPED BASS About half of a fish's body is made up of the muscles it uses for swimming. Like nearly all fishes, the striped bass breathes through gills. Delicate fish gills are protected by gill covers. Fishes use their noses for smelling, not breathing. The lateral line runs on each side of a fish's body. It helps a fish sense movements in the water. A bony fish's swim bladder can fill with gas, which helps the fish rise or hang in the water. Scales cover the bodies of most fishes. Some scales are smooth; others are spiny with comblike edges.

backbone

skull

Most fishes, like this perch, have skeletons made of bone. Sharks and some other fishes have skeletons made of softer, lighter cartilage.

lateral line

A coelacanth's entire body is covered by heavy scales. Fossils show that coelacanths have lived on the earth for millions of years.

Ratfishes live near the sea floor, grinding up boneless animals such as sea stars for food. Many ratfishes have a poisonous spine. Like sharks, they have skeletons made of cartilage.

gill cover

poisonous spine

49

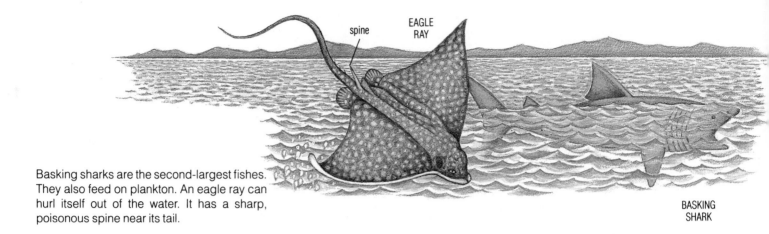

spine

EAGLE RAY

Basking sharks are the second-largest fishes. They also feed on plankton. An eagle ray can hurl itself out of the water. It has a sharp, poisonous spine near its tail.

BASKING SHARK

A fish's brain works body muscles to carefully control how and where the fish swims.

For hours on end, a fish can cruise through the water. But it may have to swim at top speed if it senses danger or locates food. A tuna cruises at 10 miles per hour (16 kilometers per hour); however, for a short time, it can slice through the water at more than 40 miles per hour (64 kph). Fast swimmers, such as tunas, usually have torpedo-shaped bodies, perfect for cutting through water.

Very few fishes swim as fast as tunas and swordfish. Most, in fact, swim at a speed of only a few miles per hour. Some fishes, such as sea robins, hardly swim at all. They walk on their fins along the sea floor.

Gills and Swim Bladders

The more active a fish is, the more oxygen it needs. Fishes can use up almost half of their energy getting enough oxygen to keep their muscles working properly.

As they swim, most fishes take water into their mouths but don't swallow it. Instead, they force the water through their gills. In a fish's gills, oxygen is soaked up by the fish's blood. At the same time, the blood releases some body wastes into the water. Carrying these wastes, the water is forced out through gill openings on each side of the fish's body.

Fish gills are fragile. Nearly all fishes would die on land, for their gills would collapse and dry up.

A fish's body is heavier than water. Even so, most fishes don't sink when they stop swimming. This is because inside them is a sac called a swim bladder. The swim bladder can fill with gas that comes out of a fish's blood. By filling its swim bladder with gas, a fish can make its body lighter. Removing some gas from its swim bladder, a fish makes its body heavier. By changing how much gas is in its swim bladder, a fish can rise, sink, or hang in the water.

The deeper a fish swims, the more forcefully the water presses against it. Fishes have to be careful not to swim so deep that the water pressure crushes them.

The whale shark, 60 feet (18 m) long, is the largest fish. Although it has many teeth, it feeds only on plankton and small fishes.

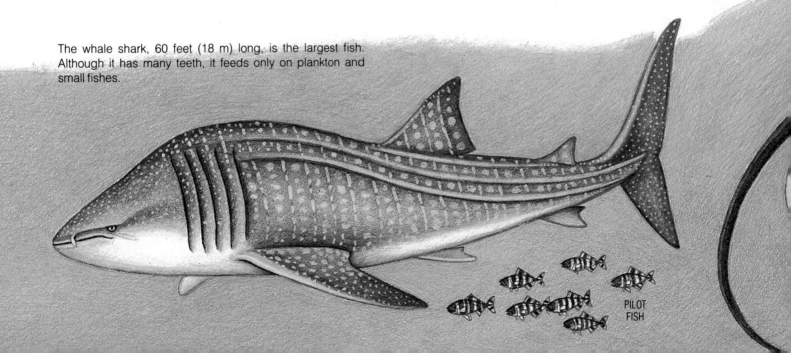

PILOT FISH

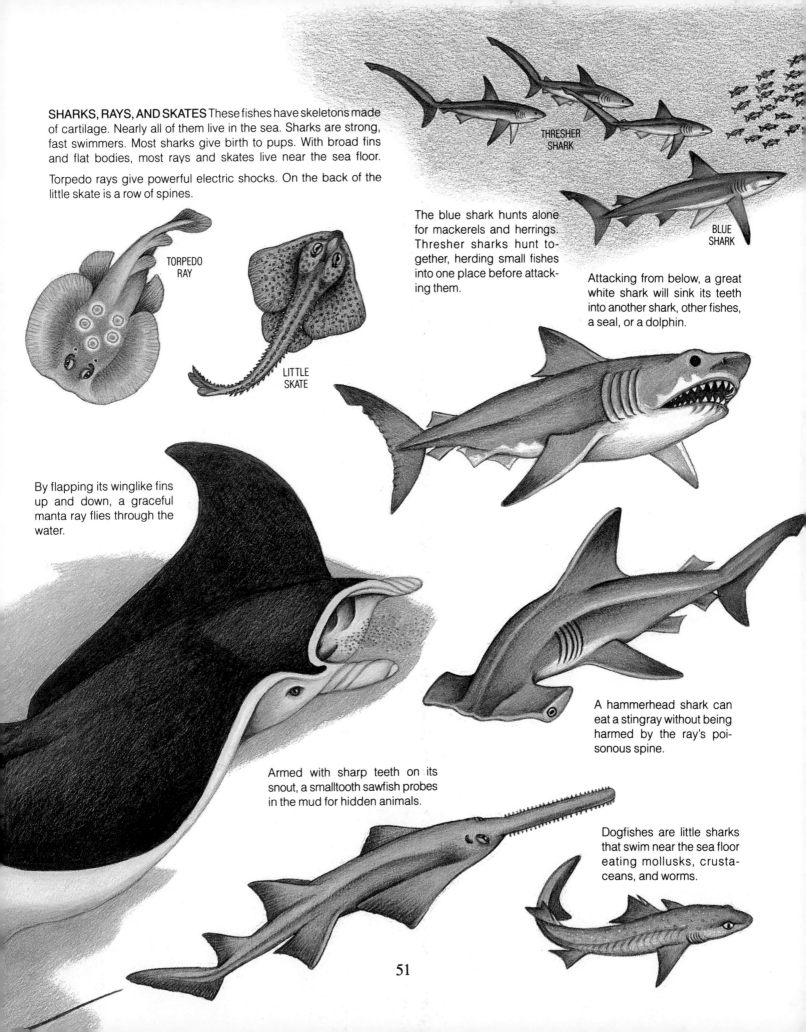

SHARKS, RAYS, AND SKATES These fishes have skeletons made of cartilage. Nearly all of them live in the sea. Sharks are strong, fast swimmers. Most sharks give birth to pups. With broad fins and flat bodies, most rays and skates live near the sea floor.

Torpedo rays give powerful electric shocks. On the back of the little skate is a row of spines.

THRESHER SHARK

TORPEDO RAY

LITTLE SKATE

The blue shark hunts alone for mackerels and herrings. Thresher sharks hunt together, herding small fishes into one place before attacking them.

BLUE SHARK

Attacking from below, a great white shark will sink its teeth into another shark, other fishes, a seal, or a dolphin.

By flapping its winglike fins up and down, a graceful manta ray flies through the water.

A hammerhead shark can eat a stingray without being harmed by the ray's poisonous spine.

Armed with sharp teeth on its snout, a smalltooth sawfish probes in the mud for hidden animals.

Dogfishes are little sharks that swim near the sea floor eating mollusks, crustaceans, and worms.

51

When a fish's body senses the pressure increasing, it starts filling its swim bladder with gas. The gas helps lift the fish back to where the pressure is safe.

Not all fishes have a swim bladder. Sharks, for example, don't have one. For this reason, sharks have to swim all the time or they sink. Flounders and other flatfishes don't have a swim bladder either. They spend their lives on the sea floor.

A few kinds of fishes, such as lungfishes, can use their swim bladders for breathing air. When these fishes need to, they swim to the surface and gulp in air. Their swim bladders work like lungs, taking oxygen out of the air they breathe.

There are more than 21,000 species of fishes. Over half live in the oceans. The others live in rivers, streams, lakes, and ponds. A few kinds of fishes, such as salmon and eels, live part of their lives in salt water and part in fresh water (page 56).

Some fishes live in warm, tropical waters, whereas others live in cool, even icy waters. Fishes can't make their own heat. The temperature inside a fish's body is nearly the same as the temperature of the water around it. One kind of fish may swim near the sunlit surface. Another kind may live in very deep, dark sea waters where the temperature remains near freezing all year round.

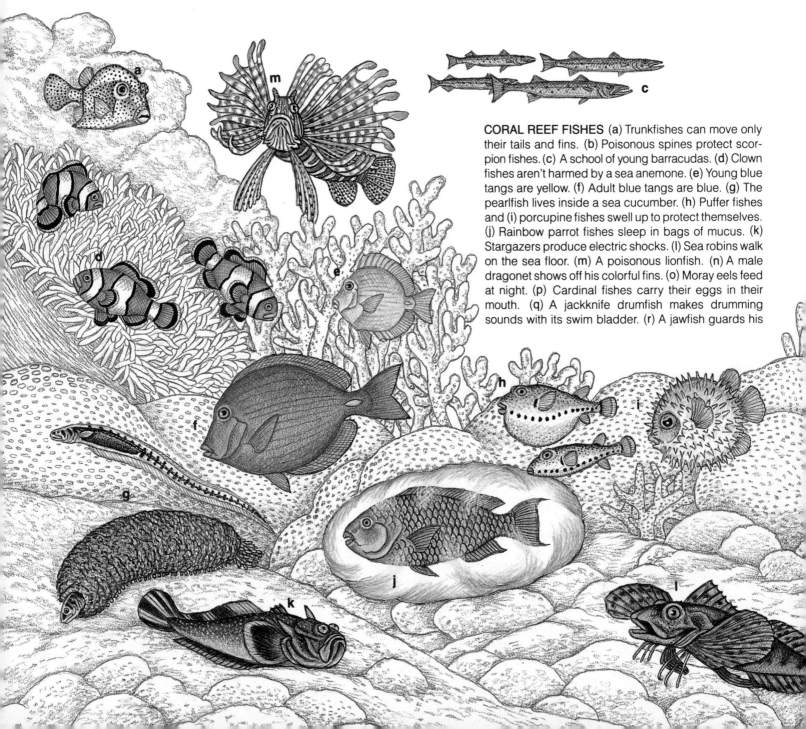

CORAL REEF FISHES (a) Trunkfishes can move only their tails and fins. (b) Poisonous spines protect scorpion fishes. (c) A school of young barracudas. (d) Clown fishes aren't harmed by a sea anemone. (e) Young blue tangs are yellow. (f) Adult blue tangs are blue. (g) The pearlfish lives inside a sea cucumber. (h) Puffer fishes and (i) porcupine fishes swell up to protect themselves. (j) Rainbow parrot fishes sleep in bags of mucus. (k) Stargazers produce electric shocks. (l) Sea robins walk on the sea floor. (m) A poisonous lionfish. (n) A male dragonet shows off his colorful fins. (o) Moray eels feed at night. (p) Cardinal fishes carry their eggs in their mouth. (q) A jackknife drumfish makes drumming sounds with its swim bladder. (r) A jawfish guards his

Fish Scales

Except over their head and fins, the bodies of most fishes are covered by tough, flexible scales. As a fish grows, its scales get larger too. Growing close to one another on top of a shark's skin are very hard scales that are like tiny teeth. Nearly all bony fishes have thin, tough, bony scales that overlap one another like shingles on a roof. On top of these bony scales grows a thin layer of skin. And out from the skin comes a slippery, slimy mucus that helps fishes move more easily through the water. The mucus also protects the skin from infection.

Although most fishes swim alone, thousands of fish species swim in schools. Some fishes travel in small schools. Others, such as herrings, travel in schools that can stretch over a mile (1.6 km). In such a school, more than 100 million herrings swim together. Almost all the fish in the school swim in the same direction and evenly spaced apart. When the school leader tires, it moves back and another fish takes its place. By schooling, the fish help protect one another. When it is time to rest, the fish in a school scatter. Later they regroup and continue on their way.

Because they have no eyelids, most fishes rest with their eyes open. Water constantly bathes a fish's eyes. Some fishes rest on their sides or buried in the sand.

territory. (s) The male northern pipefish carries eggs in his pouch until they hatch. (t) This yellow-headed wrasse is being cleaned by a small shark-nosed goby. (u) Butterfly fishes poke among coral looking for food. (v) Groupers can weigh 600 pounds (270 kg). (w) Filefishes have tiny, hard scales. (x) As it swims, a French angelfish weaves back and forth. (y) Leafy sea dragons look like floating seaweed. (z) The surgeonfish lifts its spine when it is excited.

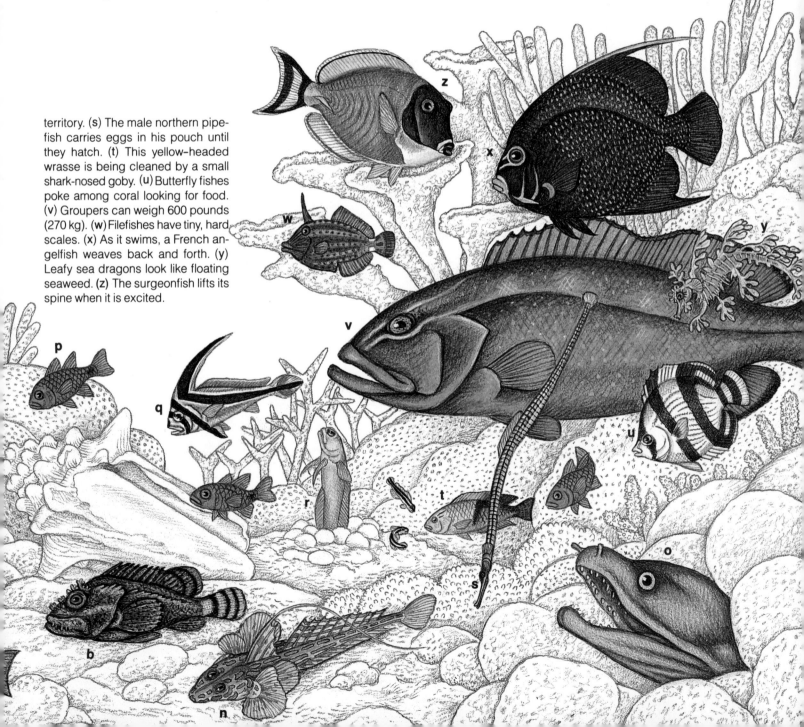

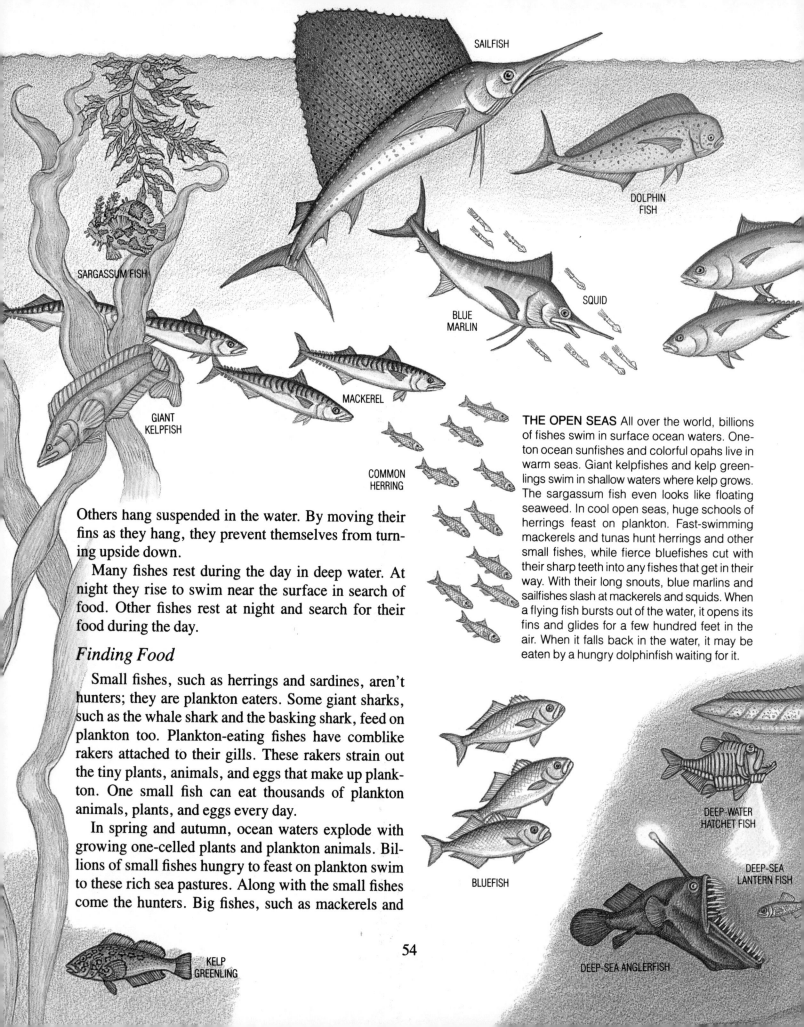

Others hang suspended in the water. By moving their fins as they hang, they prevent themselves from turning upside down.

Many fishes rest during the day in deep water. At night they rise to swim near the surface in search of food. Other fishes rest at night and search for their food during the day.

Finding Food

Small fishes, such as herrings and sardines, aren't hunters; they are plankton eaters. Some giant sharks, such as the whale shark and the basking shark, feed on plankton too. Plankton-eating fishes have comblike rakers attached to their gills. These rakers strain out the tiny plants, animals, and eggs that make up plankton. One small fish can eat thousands of plankton animals, plants, and eggs every day.

In spring and autumn, ocean waters explode with growing one-celled plants and plankton animals. Billions of small fishes hungry to feast on plankton swim to these rich sea pastures. Along with the small fishes come the hunters. Big fishes, such as mackerels and

THE OPEN SEAS All over the world, billions of fishes swim in surface ocean waters. One-ton ocean sunfishes and colorful opahs live in warm seas. Giant kelpfishes and kelp greenlings swim in shallow waters where kelp grows. The sargassum fish even looks like floating seaweed. In cool open seas, huge schools of herrings feast on plankton. Fast-swimming mackerels and tunas hunt herrings and other small fishes, while fierce bluefishes cut with their sharp teeth into any fishes that get in their way. With their long snouts, blue marlins and sailfishes slash at mackerels and squids. When a flying fish bursts out of the water, it opens its fins and glides for a few hundred feet in the air. When it falls back in the water, it may be eaten by a hungry dolphinfish waiting for it.

54

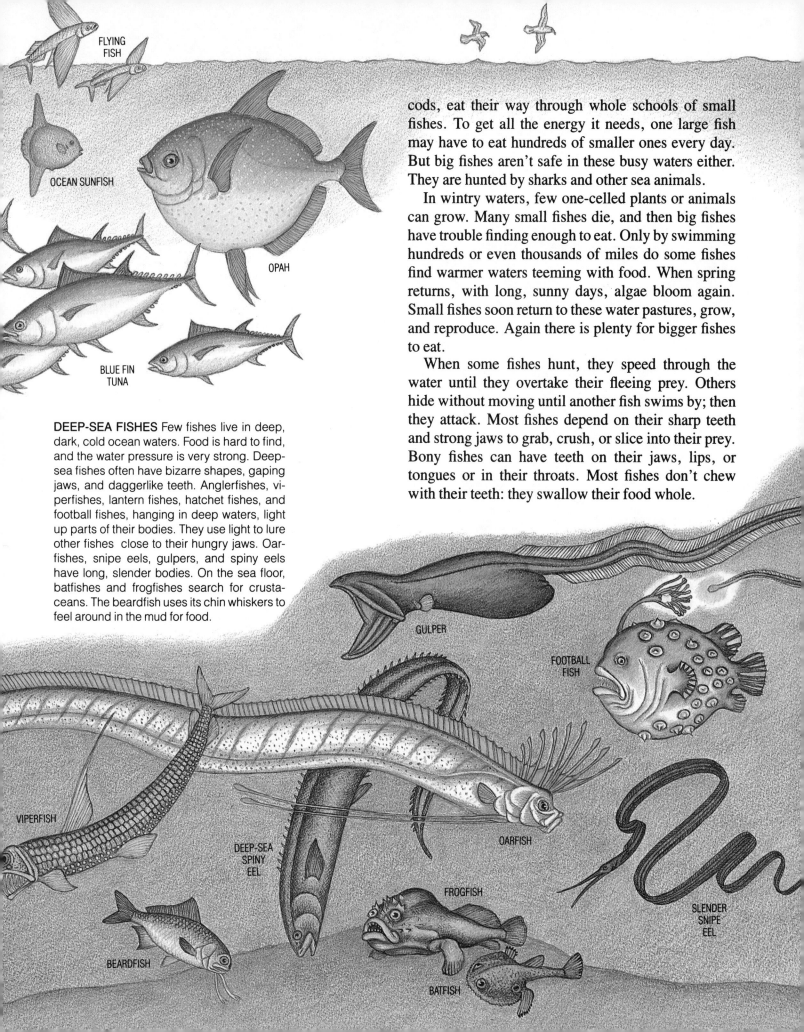

FLYING
FISH

OCEAN SUNFISH

OPAH

BLUE FIN
TUNA

DEEP-SEA FISHES Few fishes live in deep, dark, cold ocean waters. Food is hard to find, and the water pressure is very strong. Deep-sea fishes often have bizarre shapes, gaping jaws, and daggerlike teeth. Anglerfishes, viperfishes, lantern fishes, hatchet fishes, and football fishes, hanging in deep waters, light up parts of their bodies. They use light to lure other fishes close to their hungry jaws. Oarfishes, snipe eels, gulpers, and spiny eels have long, slender bodies. On the sea floor, batfishes and frogfishes search for crustaceans. The beardfish uses its chin whiskers to feel around in the mud for food.

cods, eat their way through whole schools of small fishes. To get all the energy it needs, one large fish may have to eat hundreds of smaller ones every day. But big fishes aren't safe in these busy waters either. They are hunted by sharks and other sea animals.

In wintry waters, few one-celled plants or animals can grow. Many small fishes die, and then big fishes have trouble finding enough to eat. Only by swimming hundreds or even thousands of miles do some fishes find warmer waters teeming with food. When spring returns, with long, sunny days, algae bloom again. Small fishes soon return to these water pastures, grow, and reproduce. Again there is plenty for bigger fishes to eat.

When some fishes hunt, they speed through the water until they overtake their fleeing prey. Others hide without moving until another fish swims by; then they attack. Most fishes depend on their sharp teeth and strong jaws to grab, crush, or slice into their prey. Bony fishes can have teeth on their jaws, lips, or tongues or in their throats. Most fishes don't chew with their teeth: they swallow their food whole.

GULPER

FOOTBALL
FISH

VIPERFISH

DEEP-SEA
SPINY
EEL

OARFISH

FROGFISH

SLENDER
SNIPE
EEL

BEARDFISH

BATFISH

SALMON MIGRATION For years, adult Pacific salmon live in the ocean, growing large by eating small fishes such as herrings. When it is time for them to mate, they return to the same freshwater stream where they hatched from eggs. Some salmon migrate more than 2,000 miles (3,200 km) to reach their destinations. Along the way many are eaten by sharks, other large fishes, and seabirds.

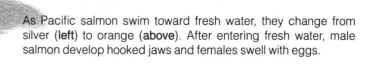

female

male

As Pacific salmon swim toward fresh water, they change from silver (**left**) to orange (**above**). After entering fresh water, male salmon develop hooked jaws and females swell with eggs.

EUROPEAN EEL

ATLANTIC OCEAN

AMERICAN EEL

American eels live in fresh water. When it is time for them to reproduce, they swim more than 1,000 miles (1,600 km) to the Sargasso Sea off Bermuda. After laying millions of eggs, the adult eels die. Once the eggs hatch, it takes more than a year for the baby eels to make their way back to North America. The young elvers return to the same waters where their parents lived, even though they were never there before. As the map shows, European eels make a similar journey to the Sargasso Sea.

elver

Sharks are among the most expert hunters in the animal world. Most hunt alone, but thresher sharks hunt in groups. Led on by their extraordinary sense of smell and taste, sharks pick up chemical trails in the water, which lead them to prey. If a shark is hurt, other sharks will turn on it, attack, and even eat it. Most sharks have rows of sharp, triangle-shaped cutting teeth on their strong jaws. New teeth keep growing to take the place of lost ones.

Near the sea floor live many fishes that eat mollusks, crustaceans, or worms. Some of these fishes use their long snouts to suck up mud. From the mud, the fishes strain out tiny animals, wastes, or parts of dead animals they can use for food.

In deep, dark, cold ocean waters, where the pressure is the greatest, very few fishes are able to live. Often these deep-sea fishes have bizarre shapes, daggerlike teeth, and wide, gaping jaws. Some are scavengers, eating dead animal bodies that slowly rain down on them from above. Others hover in the water, lighting up parts of their bodies. The lights can lure other fishes close enough to be trapped in the gaping jaws of these hungry fishes. Some deep-sea fishes have special cells

The sturgeon lives part of its life in estuaries, where rivers meet the sea.

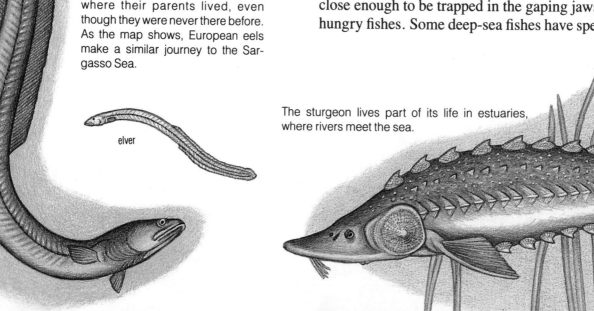

The trip upstream can be very difficult. To get past rushing rapids or waterfalls, salmon leap out of the water. Hungry bears and fishermen catch many salmon.

After their long journey, Pacific salmon are tired. They pair off and dig nests in the gravel for their eggs. Once the eggs are fertilized, both parents die.

that produce light. Others have pouches filled with bacteria that give off light. Using a flap of its skin, a fish can cover up the light so that it does not shine.

Fishes are in danger almost everywhere. Near the ocean surface they are attacked from the water below by other fishes and also from the sky above by hungry birds. Many surface swimmers are dark colored on top and light colored on their bellies. This coloring makes them harder to spot from above and from below.

Fishes swimming near the sea floor are often dark brown or black. These colors blend with the color of the mud. A few fishes, such as flounders, can change color to match the sand or rocks they rest on.

Fish Senses

Even in sunlit waters it is not easy for a fish to see clearly very far. Most fishes have eyes on the sides of their heads. Each eye works on its own, looking where it can, searching for food or for an approaching predator. Many deep-sea fishes have huge eyes, which pick up any light that breaks the near-total darkness. Only a few fishes are blind.

Fishes have no difficulty swimming in the dark

eggs

When the salmon hatch, they have a food sac of egg yolk still attached to them. But after a few weeks the young salmon hunt on their own. For two years they live in rivers. Then they turn silver and swim downstream to the ocean.

food sac

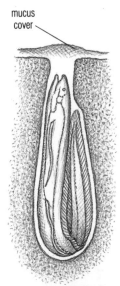

mucus cover

AFRICAN LUNGFISH

The four-eyed fish really has only two eyes. Each eye is divided into two parts. While the upper parts peer above the water, the lower parts peer below.

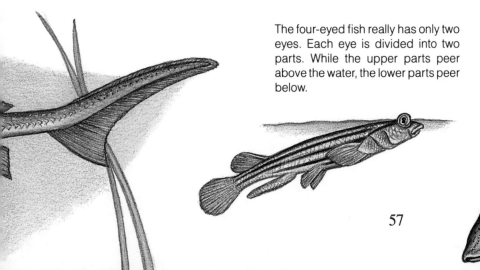

An African lungfish buries itself in the mud if its river begins to dry. It sleeps wrapped in mucus and breathes air. When the rains come, it wakes up and swims away.

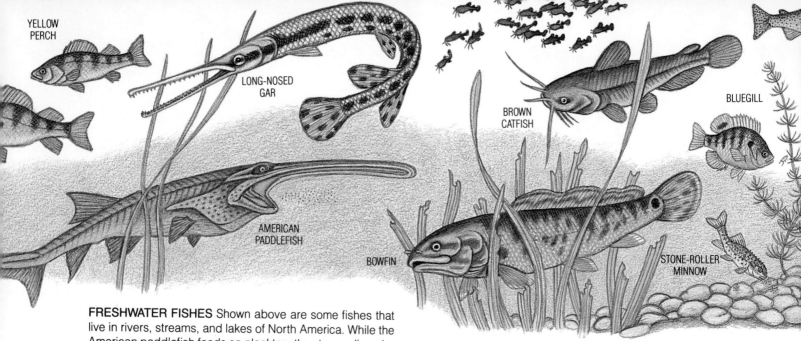

YELLOW PERCH

LONG-NOSED GAR

BROWN CATFISH

BLUEGILL

AMERICAN PADDLEFISH

BOWFIN

STONE-ROLLER MINNOW

FRESHWATER FISHES Shown above are some fishes that live in rivers, streams, and lakes of North America. While the American paddlefish feeds on plankton, the stone-roller minnow scrapes algae off rocks. Hungry rainbow trout chase silverside minnows. As yellow perches try to escape the jaws of the long-nosed gar, a bluegill hunts water insects. A northern pike, 5 feet (1.5 m) long, lurks about waiting for a tasty meal to swim by. To protect her young, a brown catfish keeps them in a group. A female bitterling lays her eggs inside the shells of a freshwater mussel while a common carp lays her eggs on plants. A male bowfin, pumpkinseed, and North American sunfish each make a nest to guard. Below are some fishes that live in warm, tropical waters. A female guppy gives birth to her babies. The upside-down catfish swims on its back. With its long snout, a freshwater elephant fish probes for worms. A male discus fish directs his stray babies back to their mother. A male green swordtail shows off his colors. An electric eel may stun a small fish with an electric shock. The banded knifefish can move backward or forward. By squirting drops out of the water, an archer fish can shoot down an insect on a plant. A male pearl gourami guards the eggs in the bubble nest he has blown around them. Using their razor-sharp teeth, red-bellied piranhas can cut another animal into pieces. A bichir walks along on its front fins. A school of cardinal tetras darts about. Both Indian climbing perches and mudskippers can come on land for a short time.

because of their lateral line. The lateral line runs along each side of a fish's body. It feels movement in the water and helps fishes tell where rocks are, which way the currents are flowing, and how to swim without crashing into anything. It also alerts a fish to any movement nearby. In a school, each fish's lateral line helps it stay just the right distance away from the other fishes swimming nearby.

When fishes sense danger, they can try to speed away through the water to a safer spot. If attacked, fishes use their jaws and any other weapons they have, such as poisonous spines, to defend themselves. Torpedo rays and some eels have a powerful weapon in the electricity their bodies make and store. This electricity can produce a shock strong enough to stun or kill another animal.

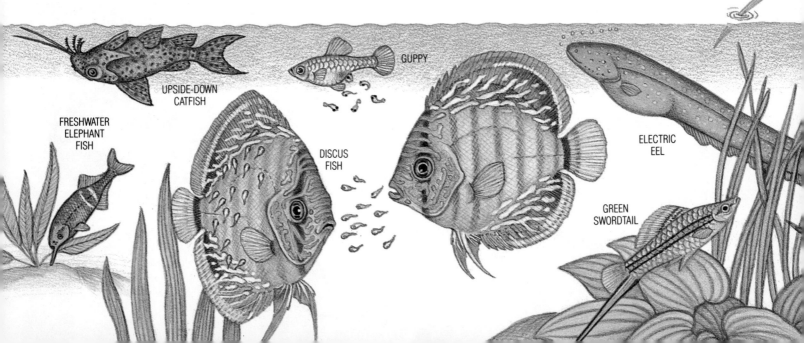

GUPPY

UPSIDE-DOWN CATFISH

FRESHWATER ELEPHANT FISH

DISCUS FISH

ELECTRIC EEL

GREEN SWORDTAIL

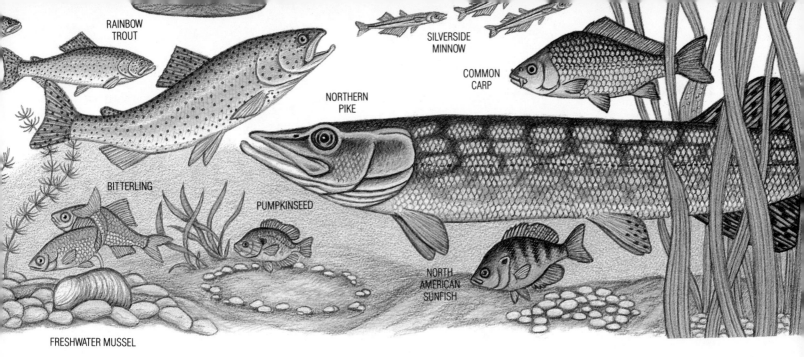

RAINBOW TROUT

SILVERSIDE MINNOW

NORTHERN PIKE

COMMON CARP

BITTERLING

PUMPKINSEED

NORTH AMERICAN SUNFISH

FRESHWATER MUSSEL

From Eggs to Fishes

Every day millions of fishes are eaten by other fishes, birds, and mammals. Even so, the waters remain full of fishes because of the vast numbers of young that fishes produce.

At mating, most fishes release millions of eggs or sperm into the water. The fertilized eggs of some fishes float in the plankton. Other fertilized eggs sink or stick to plants and rocks.

Some freshwater fishes dig nests of mud or sand for their eggs. Others, such as certain catfishes, hold their eggs in their mouths until the eggs hatch.

Many sharks and some bony fishes, such as guppies, keep their eggs inside their bodies until hatching. Then their young are born alive. Sea horses have a very unusual way of reproducing. The female sea horse lays her eggs inside a pouch on the male's body. He carries the eggs until the tiny sea horses hatch.

Most newborn fishes are transparent and scaleless, and float in the plankton. Very many are eaten. Others drift where they can't survive. Often baby fishes have a food sac attached to their bodies (page 57). As they slowly develop, they use up this food and then swim off to hunt on their own.

Only a very few fishes ever leave the water. Flying fishes can leap out of the water and glide through the air for a short distance. But they always return underwater. Mudskippers can flop onto land for a short period of time. On land, they skip along, searching for insects. But they never move far from the water. Some eels also come on land. They wriggle through damp grasses as they move from one pond to another.

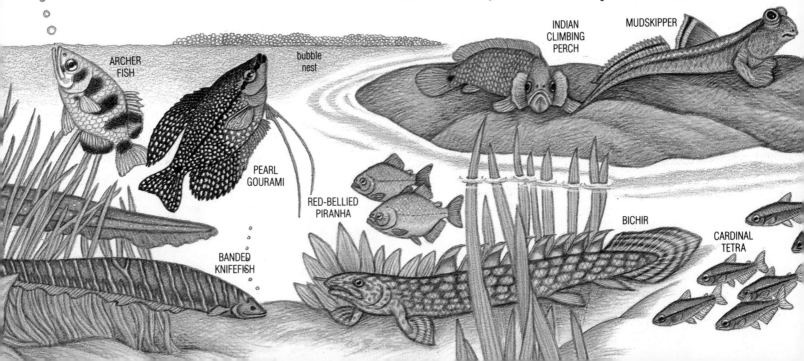

ARCHER FISH

bubble nest

INDIAN CLIMBING PERCH

MUDSKIPPER

PEARL GOURAMI

RED-BELLIED PIRANHA

BICHIR

CARDINAL TETRA

BANDED KNIFEFISH

Amphibians

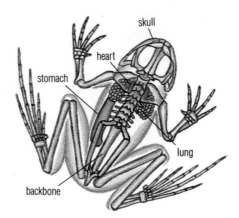

Like all adult amphibians, frogs have bony skeletons. Frogs breathe through their lungs and their thin skin. On top of a frog's head are its bulging eyes. A frog's eyes can see above, behind, in front, and to the side at the same time. Frogs use their long, muscular back legs for jumping.

IN THE SPRING, many kinds of frogs leap along until they reach a pond, where they will breed. Usually, the male frogs arrive first. Each male calls out with his croaking song, hoping to attract a female. Throat sacs help make these calls strong enough to carry a long way. All the different male frogs singing together create a loud croaking chorus. As the female frogs arrive, each female picks out the call of a male belonging to her species.

When they are ready to mate, the male frog holds on to the female's back using special leg pads he grows. As the female releases a few thousand eggs into the water, the male quickly releases his sperm over them. Then both frogs leave the eggs.

In the water, the jelly around the eggs swells and hardens. Many of the eggs are eaten by water insects, fishes, and snakes. But inside most of the other eggs a tadpole develops until it is ready to hatch.

Moving their tails from side to side, tadpoles swim, feeding on freshwater plants. Like fishes, they breathe through gills. They also have a lateral line for sensing the world around them. After a few weeks of growth, tadpoles start to develop legs and lungs. By the time a tadpole is three months old, many changes have taken place. Its gills and tail have disappeared, it has shed its skin, and it no longer eats plants. The metamorphosis is complete: the tadpole has become a frog. It is ready to live and breathe on land.

On land, a frog first catches insects with its moist, sticky tongue. As it grows older, it also catches snails, beetles, spiders, and worms. When a frog feels cold, it has to rest in the sun to absorb heat. If it gets too warm, it moves into the shade or cools off in water. In winter, many frogs sleep buried in the mud at the bottom of a pond. With their mouths, eyes, and nostrils closed, these hibernating frogs breathe through their skin. Only when a frog is three years old is it ready to mate.

Animals such as frogs are called amphibians because they lead a double life. Nearly all amphibians live the first part of their lives underwater. Then they change into adults able to live and breathe on land. Amphibians have strong, flexible backbones, which support their

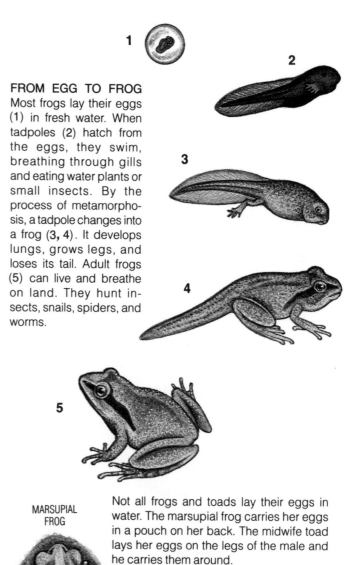

FROM EGG TO FROG
Most frogs lay their eggs (1) in fresh water. When tadpoles (2) hatch from the eggs, they swim, breathing through gills and eating water plants or small insects. By the process of metamorphosis, a tadpole changes into a frog (3, 4). It develops lungs, grows legs, and loses its tail. Adult frogs (5) can live and breathe on land. They hunt insects, snails, spiders, and worms.

Not all frogs and toads lay their eggs in water. The marsupial frog carries her eggs in a pouch on her back. The midwife toad lays her eggs on the legs of the male and he carries them around.

MARSUPIAL FROG

MALE MIDWIFE TOAD

eggs

eggs

FROGS AND TOADS There are more than 2,600 species of frogs and toads. Frogs and toads are similar, but toads usually have shorter legs. Whereas frogs leap, toads make short hops. Toads don't have to live as close to water as frogs do. They have thicker skin, which helps them keep in body water.

On hot, dry days, desert spadefoot toads burrow underground.

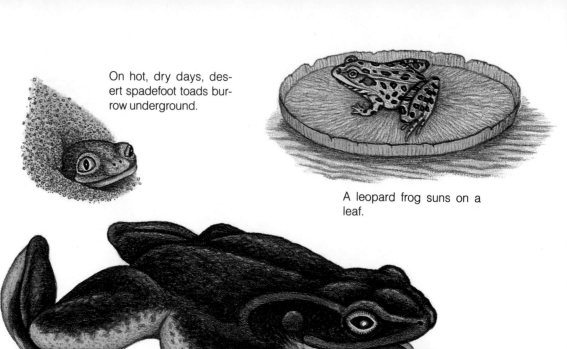

A leopard frog suns on a leaf.

A goliath frog, 12 inches (30 cm) long, flicks out its sticky tongue to catch an insect. A frog's tongue is attached to the front of its mouth.

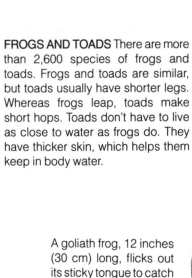

The poison dart frog (**below**) and the poisonous blue Surinam toad have bright colors that warn predators to keep away.

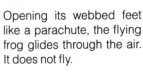

On the forest floor, a leaf toad's colors blend in with the dead leaves.

Opening its webbed feet like a parachute, the flying frog glides through the air. It does not fly.

COMMON TOAD

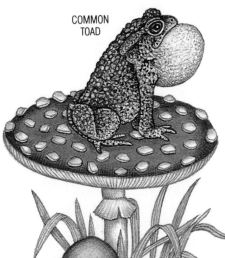

To attract females, a male common toad and a spring peeper frog call with their songs.

SPRING PEEPER FROG

A bullfrog jumps with its powerful hind legs. It also uses its webbed feet like flippers for swimming.

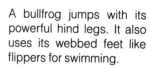

This red-eyed tree frog has suction pads on its feet.

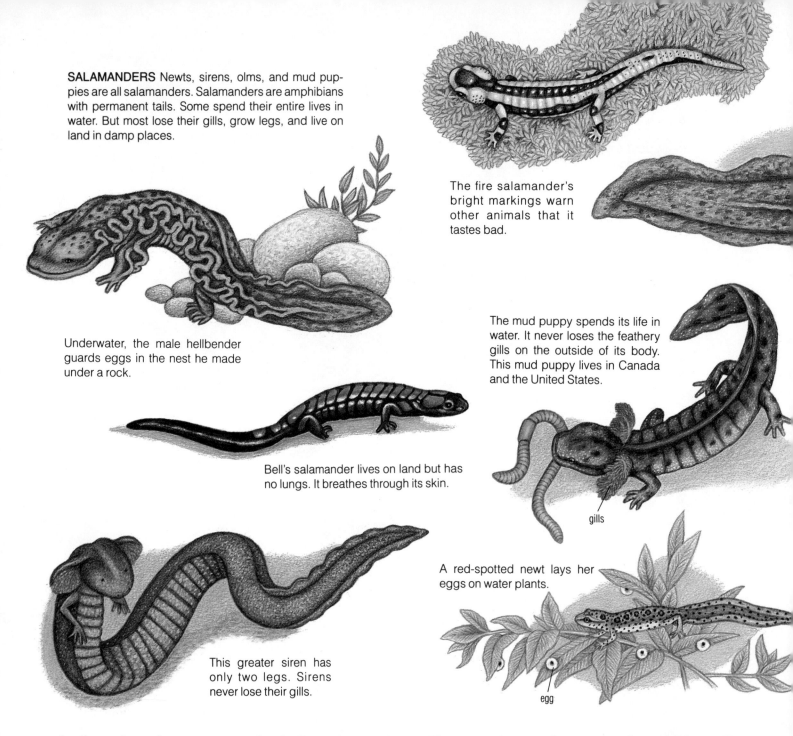

SALAMANDERS Newts, sirens, olms, and mud puppies are all salamanders. Salamanders are amphibians with permanent tails. Some spend their entire lives in water. But most lose their gills, grow legs, and live on land in damp places.

The fire salamander's bright markings warn other animals that it tastes bad.

Underwater, the male hellbender guards eggs in the nest he made under a rock.

The mud puppy spends its life in water. It never loses the feathery gills on the outside of its body. This mud puppy lives in Canada and the United States.

gills

Bell's salamander lives on land but has no lungs. It breathes through its skin.

A red-spotted newt lays her eggs on water plants.

This greater siren has only two legs. Sirens never lose their gills.

egg

bodies when they move on land. Just about all amphibians also have smooth, thin, moist skin without any scales to protect it. This skin is so thin that it lets water in and out. Frogs don't have to drink, for they take in water through their skin.

An amphibian's thin skin is also used for taking in oxygen and getting rid of wastes. Skin glands produce mucus to help keep the skin moist out of water. If their skin dries out, amphibians die. For this reason some amphibians have to live in or near fresh water. Others can live in the moist air of damp woods and tropical forests.

There are three main groups of amphibians. The largest group is made up of the more than 2,600 species of frogs and toads. Toads are similar to frogs, but they usually have shorter legs and thicker, drier skin than frogs. A thicker skin helps toads live farther away from water than frogs can.

More than 300 species of salamanders form the second group of amphibians. They hatch with tails that are permanent. Like frogs and toads, most salamanders start life in the water. Their gills are on the outside of their bodies. A few kinds of salamanders, such as olms, never lose their gills and spend their

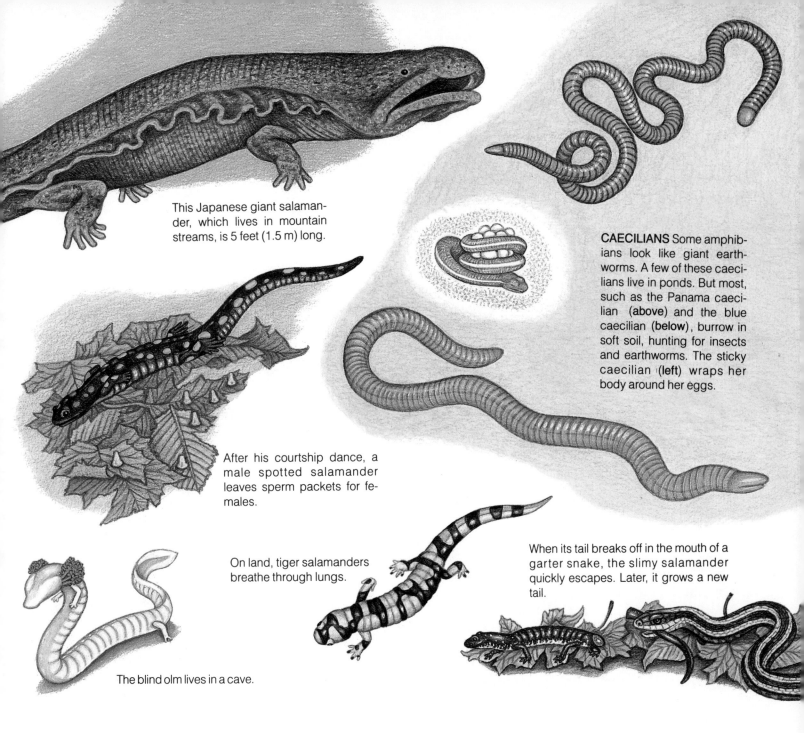

This Japanese giant salamander, which lives in mountain streams, is 5 feet (1.5 m) long.

CAECILIANS Some amphibians look like giant earthworms. A few of these caecilians live in ponds. But most, such as the Panama caecilian (above) and the blue caecilian (below), burrow in soft soil, hunting for insects and earthworms. The sticky caecilian (left) wraps her body around her eggs.

After his courtship dance, a male spotted salamander leaves sperm packets for females.

On land, tiger salamanders breathe through lungs.

When its tail breaks off in the mouth of a garter snake, the slimy salamander quickly escapes. Later, it grows a new tail.

The blind olm lives in a cave.

entire lives in water. Most other salamanders lose their gills, grow legs, and live on land in moist places or in caves. While many of these salamanders grow lungs, some have no lungs or gills. As adults, they breathe through their very moist skin.

Although most salamanders try to hide from danger, some give off a poison from their skin. This poison makes nearly all animals trying to eat them spit them out. Some salamanders also have tails that break off when they are grabbed. These salamanders can escape to safety by leaving their tails behind. Later, they grow new ones.

The third group of amphibians have no legs and look like giant earthworms. They are called caecilians. There are more than 150 caecilian species. A few live in ponds and streams, moving like eels when they swim. All the rest live on land, where they often burrow in soft soil, searching for insects and earthworms to eat. Even though they have eyes, they can't see. When they hunt, they depend on special feelers to help them find their prey. Many have small scales under their slimy skin, and when they move, their bodies slither along like snakes. But snakes are not amphibians, they are reptiles.

Reptiles

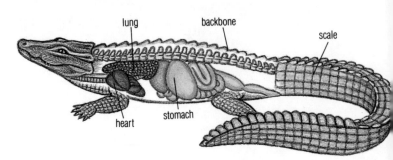

ON FOUR ISLANDS in the Far East lives the Komodo dragon. It grows to be 8 to 10 feet (2.4 to 3 m) long and can weigh 300 pounds (135 kg). With its thick tail, muscular legs, sharp claws, and large, jagged teeth it can kill a deer or a wild pig. The Komodo isn't really a dragon but a lizard. And lizards, snakes, crocodiles, and turtles are all reptiles. Dinosaurs that lived millions of years ago were reptiles too.

More than 6,200 reptile species live on land, in trees, or in water. Most reptiles have a thick skin with tough, dry scales or bony plates. Scales keep a reptile's skin dry. They also prevent water from escaping out of its body. Scales enable many reptiles to live in deserts without drying out and dying.

TURTLES

Turtles are the only living reptiles with shells. Most turtle shells are made of an inner layer of bony plates and an outer layer of scales. The bony plates are joined to the skeleton. And, at each side of the turtle's body, the upper shell attaches to the lower.

Turtles don't have teeth. They use their sharp-edged jaws to tear at the plants and animals they eat. When turtles sense danger, they may pull into their shells.

Turtles never shed their shells. As a turtle grows, its shell scales get larger and thicker. Not all turtle shells are hard. Some turtles have only a tough, leathery skin covering their bodies.

Some turtles live in the sea. Others live in fresh water or on land. Land turtles are called tortoises.

Nearly all reptiles lay their eggs on land. Even sea turtles return to land to lay their eggs. Reptile eggs have tough shells outside and plenty of food and water inside. The eggshells also let in enough oxygen for the young reptile growing inside.

After burying their eggs, most reptiles leave the eggs to develop on their own. However, alligators and crocodiles often make nests for their eggs. They not only guard the eggs but also help protect their young after hatching.

A few kinds of snakes and lizards don't lay eggs. Instead, they keep the eggs inside their bodies until their young are ready to hatch.

INSIDE AN AMERICAN ALLIGATOR Like all reptiles, the American alligator has a bony skeleton, breathes through lungs, and gets its heat from the sun. Covering its skin are thick, dry scales. When an alligator swims underwater, it closes off its nostrils and ears. Its windpipe also closes to prevent water from getting into its lungs if it grabs food.

A Nile crocodile digs a nest for her eggs, covers them with sand, and then guards them. When she hears her babies make sounds, she opens the nest so that they can crawl out. Sometimes the babies hide in her mouth.

Using its temporary egg tooth, a snapping turtle cuts its way out of the egg.

The tuatara, which lives only in New Zealand, is 2 feet (60 cm) long. It will burrow underground to escape danger.

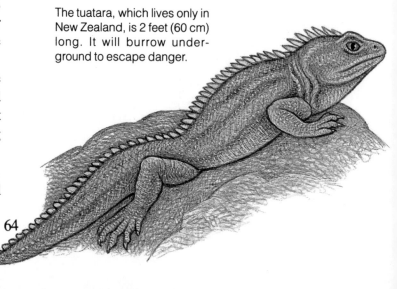

64

TURTLES There are more than 200 species of turtles. They are the only living reptiles with shells. The upper part of the shell is called the carapace. The plastron is the shell part underneath a turtle's body. Turtles live in the sea, in fresh water, or on land. To swim, sea turtles move their paddlelike flippers like oars.

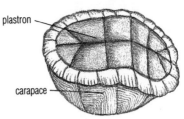

plastron

carapace

To hide, an American box turtle can pull all of its head, legs, and tail back into its shell. Not all turtles can do this.

Tortoises are land turtles. This plant-eating Galápagos giant tortoise, which may live 150 years, weighs 500 pounds (225 kg).

Leatherback sea turtles paddle along, hunting jellyfishes. These turtles have thin shells covered by heavy skin.

lure

An unsuspecting fish is attracted to the pink, fleshy lure in the mouth of an alligator snapping turtle.

(1) After swimming hundreds of miles to the beach where she hatched from an egg, a green sea turtle uses her flippers to pull herself along the sand. (2) When she finds a spot that the water won't reach, she digs a deep hole and lays her eggs in it. After covering the eggs with sand, she returns to the sea, leaving them to be kept warm by the sun. (3) In about two months the eggs hatch and the baby turtles dig out of their nest. (4) Immediately, they scramble for the sea before hungry seabirds or beach animals eat them.

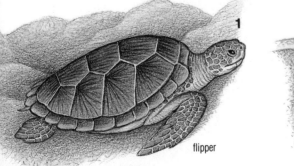
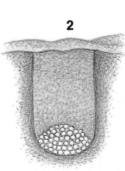

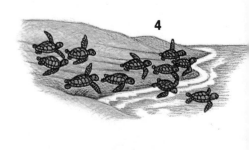

1

flipper

2

3

4

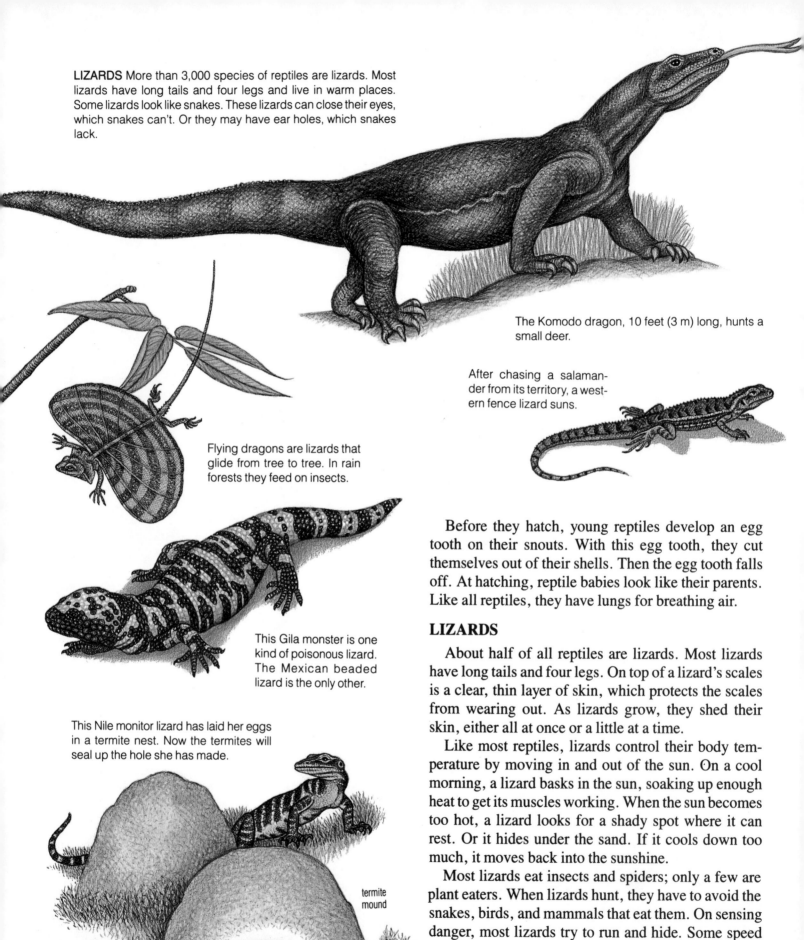

LIZARDS More than 3,000 species of reptiles are lizards. Most lizards have long tails and four legs and live in warm places. Some lizards look like snakes. These lizards can close their eyes, which snakes can't. Or they may have ear holes, which snakes lack.

The Komodo dragon, 10 feet (3 m) long, hunts a small deer.

After chasing a salamander from its territory, a western fence lizard suns.

Flying dragons are lizards that glide from tree to tree. In rain forests they feed on insects.

This Gila monster is one kind of poisonous lizard. The Mexican beaded lizard is the only other.

This Nile monitor lizard has laid her eggs in a termite nest. Now the termites will seal up the hole she has made.

termite mound

eggs

Before they hatch, young reptiles develop an egg tooth on their snouts. With this egg tooth, they cut themselves out of their shells. Then the egg tooth falls off. At hatching, reptile babies look like their parents. Like all reptiles, they have lungs for breathing air.

LIZARDS

About half of all reptiles are lizards. Most lizards have long tails and four legs. On top of a lizard's scales is a clear, thin layer of skin, which protects the scales from wearing out. As lizards grow, they shed their skin, either all at once or a little at a time.

Like most reptiles, lizards control their body temperature by moving in and out of the sun. On a cool morning, a lizard basks in the sun, soaking up enough heat to get its muscles working. When the sun becomes too hot, a lizard looks for a shady spot where it can rest. Or it hides under the sand. If it cools down too much, it moves back into the sunshine.

Most lizards eat insects and spiders; only a few are plant eaters. When lizards hunt, they have to avoid the snakes, birds, and mammals that eat them. On sensing danger, most lizards try to run and hide. Some speed

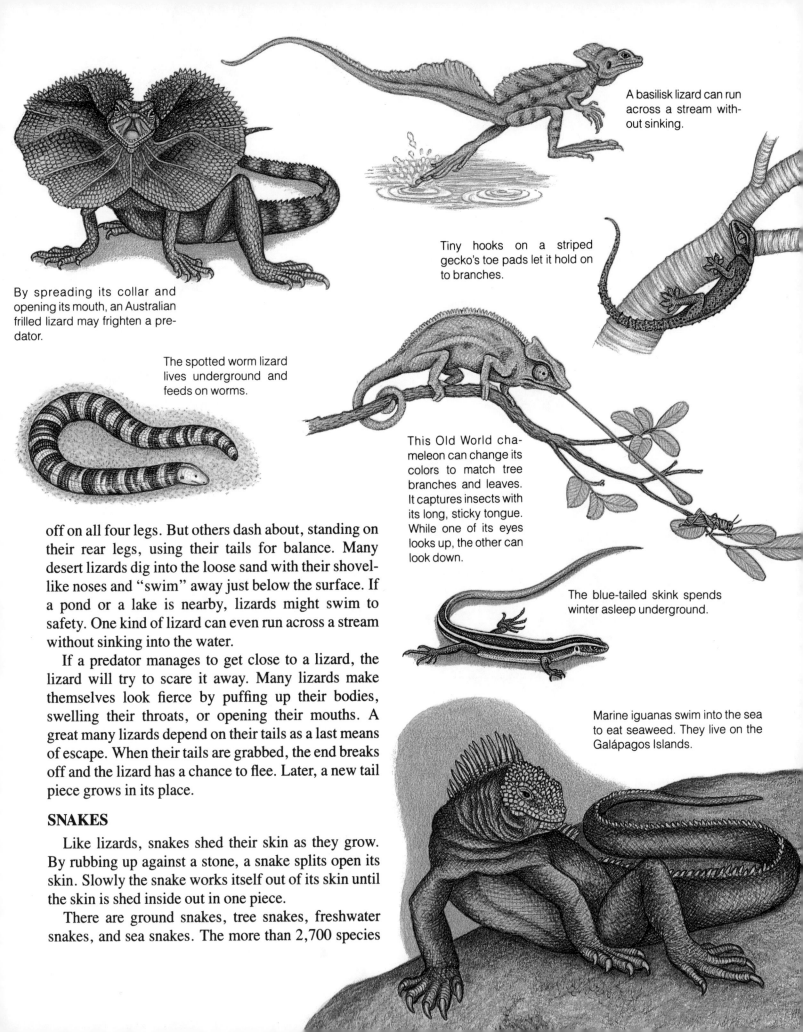

A basilisk lizard can run across a stream without sinking.

Tiny hooks on a striped gecko's toe pads let it hold on to branches.

By spreading its collar and opening its mouth, an Australian frilled lizard may frighten a predator.

The spotted worm lizard lives underground and feeds on worms.

This Old World chameleon can change its colors to match tree branches and leaves. It captures insects with its long, sticky tongue. While one of its eyes looks up, the other can look down.

The blue-tailed skink spends winter asleep underground.

Marine iguanas swim into the sea to eat seaweed. They live on the Galápagos Islands.

off on all four legs. But others dash about, standing on their rear legs, using their tails for balance. Many desert lizards dig into the loose sand with their shovel-like noses and "swim" away just below the surface. If a pond or a lake is nearby, lizards might swim to safety. One kind of lizard can even run across a stream without sinking into the water.

If a predator manages to get close to a lizard, the lizard will try to scare it away. Many lizards make themselves look fierce by puffing up their bodies, swelling their throats, or opening their mouths. A great many lizards depend on their tails as a last means of escape. When their tails are grabbed, the end breaks off and the lizard has a chance to flee. Later, a new tail piece grows in its place.

SNAKES

Like lizards, snakes shed their skin as they grow. By rubbing up against a stone, a snake splits open its skin. Slowly the snake works itself out of its skin until the skin is shed inside out in one piece.

There are ground snakes, tree snakes, freshwater snakes, and sea snakes. The more than 2,700 species

SNAKES Snakes are legless reptiles that live on the ground, in trees, or in water. They hunt for other animals or for eggs, which they swallow whole. Many snakes are armed with fangs that release a deadly poison. Some snakes give birth to their young, but most lay eggs.

shed skin

After its skin splits open, a green mamba snake slowly wriggles out of it.

CORAL SNAKE

FALSE CORAL SNAKE

The false coral snake isn't poisonous. But because it wears the same colors as the poisonous coral snake, animals also stay away from it.

To keep her eggs warm, the Indian python coils around them for more than two months.

Special pits in the diamondback rattlesnake's face help it sense the heat given off by mammals and birds. A shaking rattle is a clear warning: "Stay Away."

heat pits

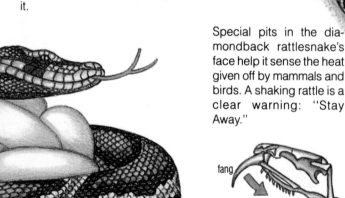

fang

Snakes have fangs in the front or back part of their mouth. Some snakes can fold back their fangs when they aren't needed.

The very poisonous yellow-bellied sea snake hunts small fishes.

have a variety of stunning patterns and colors, which help them hide or warn other animals that they are poisonous. Most snakes live alone in warm places. Others, though, live where winters are cold. These snakes hibernate underground or in caves until warm weather returns.

Even without legs, snakes can swim, climb trees, or slither just about anywhere on the ground. To move, many snakes bend their bodies from side to side, pushing off rocks, sticks, or bumps in the ground. Other snakes pull their bodies along in a straight line, using their large belly scales to catch the ground. To get across the scorching desert sand, some snakes throw their bodies along in loops.

Different snakes hunt mice, rabbits, birds, frogs, insects, lizards, and even other snakes. Snakes can lie in wait for their prey or stalk it, striking like lightning. Some snakes suffocate their prey by coiling tightly around it. Others sink their teeth into their victims. When poisonous snakes bite, their thin, sharp fang teeth release a deadly venom. Even if a bitten animal pulls away, it is too late: the poison will kill it. All the snake has to do is track its victim and wait for the poison to work.

RATTLESNAKE

KING SNAKE

By squeezing tightly, a king snake kills a rattlesnake to eat.

Jacobson's organ

A snake's forked tongue picks up odor particles given off by other animals. The tongue carries the particles into Jacobson's organ.

MONGOOSE

The egg-eating snake's jaw stretches and moves apart to take in a large egg.

When threatened, a hog-nosed snake may roll over and play dead.

Before attacking a mongoose with its long, poisonous fangs, a king cobra lifts and spreads the front part of its body. Measuring 18 feet (5.4 m) long, it is the longest poisonous snake.

Snakes track their prey with their keen sense of smell. A snake's long, forked tongue picks up odor particles from the ground or air. The tongue carries these particles into two pits in the roof of the snake's mouth. From these odors, the snake's brain can sense what animals are nearby and which to track down.

Rattlesnakes and pit vipers also have special face pits that sense heat given off by birds and mammals. In the dark, these snakes can follow a heat trail right to their unsuspecting victims.

Once a snake catches an animal, such as a mouse, it grips with its pointed, curved teeth, forcing the mouse into its mouth. A snake's lower jaw stretches and moves apart so that the snake can swallow the whole mouse. Some egg-eating snakes have sharp bones in their throat. These bones slice open the eggs as they are swallowed. After eating a big meal, a snake may not have to eat again for days.

To scare away predators, snakes hiss, open their mouths, rise up off the ground, swell up their necks, spit venom, give off foul smells, play dead, or shake their tails or rattles. If predators fail to back off, snakes attack. Often snakes are eaten by hedgehogs, mongooses, skunks, and most birds of prey.

69

Birds

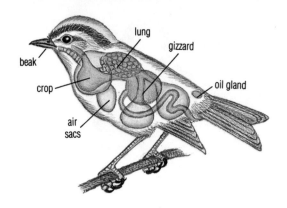

IN THE NORTH, during August and September, birds sense a change taking place. There are fewer insects to eat. The nights are cooler. Bushes and trees have started losing their leaves. For some birds the change means it will soon be winter in the place where they live all year round. But for most other birds it is a signal that soon they must fly south. There they will find plenty of food until the seasons change again.

Young birds, hatched during spring or summer, have never flown south. Yet they hatched from their eggs knowing where they must go, when to take off, and how long to wait for the wind and weather conditions best suited for flying.

Billions of birds migrate back and forth between their summer and winter homes. Many fly hundreds, even thousands of miles over mountains, forests, deserts, and oceans to reach their destinations. Their stored body fat provides them with the energy needed for such long, hazardous journeys. Many may die along the way.

Often, birds of the same species fly together in flocks. Some kinds of birds fly day and night, without stopping. They use the positions of the sun and the stars to help them find their way. Other birds fly by day or by night. Even after months of living in the north, migrating birds can land in the exact places where they spent the previous winter.

There are more than 8,600 species of birds. They range in size from hummingbirds 2 inches (5 cm) long to ostriches 7.5 feet (2.3 m) tall. Birds are the only animals in the animal world with feathers, and every bird grows them. Even birds unable to fly, such as penguins and kiwis, have feathers.

Strong, light, colored feathers grow out of a bird's skin. They protect the bird's body and keep it warm. Feathers make it possible for birds to fly.

How Birds Fly

Flying birds have lightweight bodies. Their feathers weigh little and their strong bones have many hollow spaces inside them. Instead of teeth and heavy jaws to weigh them down, birds have tough, light, toothless beaks. Beaks are also known as bills.

INSIDE A GOLDEN-CROWNED KINGLET Flying birds have light bodies and powerful flight muscles. Their strong bones are usually hollow (**right**) and their beaks and feathers weigh little. Birds are the only animals with feathers. In addition to lungs, birds have special sacs for taking in extra air. Birds can store food in their crop and grind it in their gizzard. This kinglet is a perching bird.

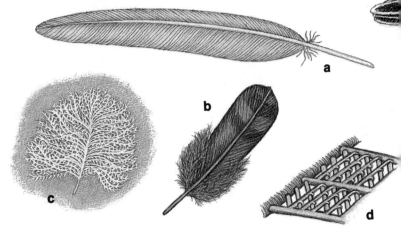

FEATHERS Long, stiff flight feathers (a) make up a bird's wings and tail. Body, or contour, feathers (b) help give a bird the best shape for flying. Soft down feathers (c) help hold in heat made by a bird's body. Flight and body feathers are made of tiny parts hooked together (d).

Clinging to a tree with its strong claws and supported by its stiff tail feathers, an acorn woodpecker (**left**) drills into bark with its powerful beak. Below, a sooty tern preens, or cares for, its feathers by pulling them through its beak.

70

For getting food, birds have different kinds of toothless beaks.

LIMPKIN

mud prober

FLAMINGO

water strainer

flesh tearer

CARACARA

seed crusher

EVENING GROSBEAK

insect trap

NIGHTJAR

a

b

c

Some birds have (a) webbed feet for swimming, (b) broad feet for walking on floating plants, or (c) clawed feet for grasping. On its long legs, a roadrunner can dash about, running at 15 miles per hour (24 kph).

WATER BIRDS Many birds live on or near water. Those with webbed feet are excellent swimmers. Birds with long legs wade into the water to hunt. And some birds spend most of their lives flying over the ocean. Shown here is a pond in spring. Flocks of mallards take off and land, and other ducks rest as they migrate north. Cranes dance wildly during courtship. Baby grebes ride on their mother's back. A swan defends its family. Loons nest, and two snow geese, mates for life, fly in to feed. While a gallinule eats snails, an American bittern senses danger, freezes in place, and points its beak up. Other water birds are illustrated on the next three pages.

WHOOPING CRANE

TRUMPETER SWAN

COMMON LOON

PURPLE GALLINULE

MALLARD

BUFFLEHEAD

SNOW GOOSE

AMERICAN BITTERN

PINTAIL

PIED GREBE

When a bird flies, it lifts itself by beating its wings up and down. At takeoff, many birds raise their wings, jump up, and launch themselves into the air. To lift itself up and forward, a flying bird beats its wings down with its powerful flight muscles. When the flight muscles relax, the wings go up and are ready to beat down again.

Most birds fly with their feet tucked in under them. To turn, birds bend and twist their wings and tail. To dive, they fold back their wings, letting their bodies drop rapidly. Birds can not only fly high and fast but also can change direction. To land, many birds break

their speed by flying into the wind, dropping their feet, spreading open their tail feathers, and tilting down their wings.

Fast fliers, such as swifts, have long, pointed wings that can carry them through the air at a speed of 100 miles per hour (160 kph). Hummingbirds can hover in the air because their very small wings can beat up to 70 times a second.

Flying uses up a lot of energy and a lot of oxygen. Birds breathe air through their lungs. In addition to lungs, birds have extra sacs, which also fill with air. These sacs help a bird get all the oxygen it needs for

TERN

STORM PETREL

ROSEATE SPOONBILL

salt marsh

A kingfisher dives for a fish.

MARIBOU STORK

With its wings raised over its head, an African black heron hunts fishes.

This American darter is sunning.

A northern jacana walks on floating plants.

GREEN HERON

flying. Air sacs also help make the bird's body light.

To save energy and rest their muscles, birds often stop beating their wings and glide along on air currents. If a gliding bird loses speed and starts dropping, it can flap its wings to regain altitude.

Some birds spend most of their flying time soaring on air currents. These large soaring birds have very large, long wings. Thousands of feet in the air, condors ride warm air currents rising up from the Andes mountains. Over the ocean, albatrosses soar for hundreds of miles on sea winds.

Feathers

Birds grow several different kinds of feathers. Long, stiff flight feathers make up a bird's wings and tail. Around the bird's body grow contour feathers, which help give the body a smooth shape for flying. Some adult birds have soft down feathers under their contour feathers. Down helps keep a bird warm.

Except for mammals, birds are the only animals that make heat inside their bodies. With this heat, they keep their body temperature between 103 and 109 degrees Fahrenheit (39–43°C) all the time.

SEABIRDS, SHOREBIRDS, AND MARSH BIRDS Above this sandy beach is a salt marsh. Both on the beach and in the marsh, birds are hunting. Spoonbills, flamingos, darters, avocets, herons, and storks hunt fishes. An oyster catcher probes the sand for oysters, and a sandpiper runs along in search of worms and small crustaceans. Over the ocean, petrels, terns, pelicans, and albatrosses fly. Skimmers slice through the water to catch fishes and other small animals in their lower beak.

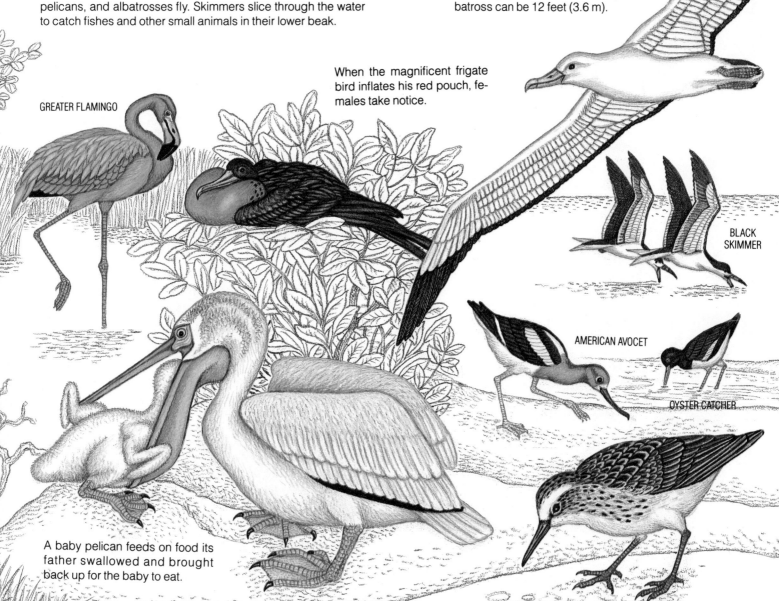

The wingspan of the wandering albatross can be 12 feet (3.6 m).

When the magnificent frigate bird inflates his red pouch, females take notice.

GREATER FLAMINGO

BLACK SKIMMER

AMERICAN AVOCET

OYSTER CATCHER

A baby pelican feeds on food its father swallowed and brought back up for the baby to eat.

WESTERN SANDPIPER

MORE SHOREBIRDS On a rocky cliff overlooking the ocean, puffins, gulls, razorbill auks, guillemots, and kittiwakes are nesting. While two blue-footed boobies court, a great skua steals a gull's egg and a black-backed gull tries to steal away a baby puffin.

PUFFIN

BLACK-BACKED GULL

BLUE-FOOTED BOOBIE

GREAT SKUA

HERRING GULL

BLACK-LEGGED KITTIWAKE

RAZORBILL AUK

BLACK GUILLEMOT

A bird can trap air under its feathers. This layer of air is warmed by the bird's body and helps prevent its heat from escaping. In cold weather, birds fluff their feathers to keep the cold out and to trap even more warmed air next to their skin.

Birds living in cold places, such as Antarctica, have lots of warm down feathers. And some swimming birds, including petrels and penguins, have a layer of fat under the skin that holds in heat.

If birds overheat, they must cool down to keep their bodies working properly. Birds can't sweat, but by panting they let some body heat escape. Some birds also flatten their contour feathers and spread apart their wing feathers to help cool off.

If feathers get dirty or sticky, they do not work well. Birds have to preen, or care for, their feathers. They also have to try to get rid of fleas and lice that feed on feathers.

Many birds bathe in streams, in puddles, or in rain. Others take dust baths. Bathing makes it easier for birds to clean and oil their feathers.

After bathing, birds use their beaks to arrange their feathers in the proper place. Each flight and contour feather is made up of many tiny parts, all hooked together. If the parts unhook, a feather starts coming apart. By pulling each feather through its beak, a bird zips the parts back together.

Most birds also oil their feathers. They dip their beaks into the oil sac near their tail and smear the oil around. Oil keeps feathers in good condition and waterproofs them. If a bird's feathers get too wet, they become so heavy that the bird can't fly.

At least once a year, adult birds shed their feathers and grow a new set. Most birds molt their flight feathers one at a time. But ducks, geese, and some other birds shed their flight feathers all at once. While their new feathers grow, these birds can't fly and have to hide from the hungry animals that hunt them.

Finding Food

Birds usually fly short distances to look for food, return to their nests, escape from danger, or find a place to rest. Most birds fly during the day, when their keen eyesight helps them find food or spot predators. Eagles and hawks see so well that from hundreds of feet in the sky they can pick out a rabbit, mouse, squirrel, or prairie dog on the ground below.

FLIGHTLESS BIRDS Although all birds have wings and feathers, some cannot fly.

A brown kiwi pokes its beak into the soft mud and finds a worm. All kiwis live in New Zealand.

crown

A flat crown protects the common cassowary's head as it moves through the forest.

skin flap

egg

When an emu over-heats, it holds out its wings to let some body heat escape.

Almost all penguins, such as these emperor penguins, live in cool Antarctic waters. Most of the year they feed at sea, paddling their small wings rapidly as they search underwater for fishes and squids. When it is time to breed, penguins swim ashore, where millions gather together. Emperor penguins gather on sea ice. After a female lays an egg, the male emperor penguin incubates it on his feet, covering it with a flap of fatty skin.

The male greater rhea sits on the eggs the female has laid on a hollow scrape in the ground. Rheas swim well and run fast.

The largest bird is the male ostrich, at 8 feet (2.4 m) tall and weighing 300 pounds (135 kg). It can run 40 miles per hour (64 kph), faster than a horse. Ostriches live on the African plains alongside hoofed mammals such as zebras. Ostriches also lay the biggest eggs, some 6 inches (15 cm) long. During the day female ostriches sit on the eggs. At night the males take over. This male, sensing danger, is ready to defend his eggs and just-hatched young.

BIRDS OF PREY With their long wings, hooked beaks, keen eyesight, strong feet, and large, sharp, curved claws (called talons), eagles, hawks, and other birds of prey are skilled flying hunters. Some birds of prey live more than 30 years.

A red-tailed hawk can see a mouse on the ground a quarter mile away.

Diving at 180 miles per hour (288 kph), a peregrine falcon swoops to capture a pigeon.

male

female

These North American bald eagles have built their nest 100 feet (30 m) above the ground. A bald eagle can force an osprey to drop a fish, then catch it before it hits the water.

Above the mountains a long-winged condor soars on warm air currents.

With its sharp, powerful talons, a harpy eagle pulls a monkey from a tree.

An osprey rises from the water, gripping a fish with its feet.

Even though secretary birds fly well, they hunt on the ground for snakes, which they stomp to death.

Long, rounded wings and soft feathers make little noise as a barn owl hunts over fields in the night.

The great horned owl hunts night and day for small mammals, snakes, frogs, and other birds. If crows or jays discover this owl, they try to drive it away.

The common poorwill is one of the few birds that hibernate through the winter.

The snowy owl nests on the ground, kept warm by its fluffy feathers.

At night, most birds rest. But night birds, such as owls, hunt. Owls have large eyes that see well in the dark. Owls also hear extremely well. In total darkness, they can pick up animal sounds and follow them.

Much of a bird's life is spent flying in search of food. Flying itself uses up so much energy that birds have to eat a lot every day. Birds also need energy to maintain their body temperature when the weather is cold or hot.

Because they fly, birds can feed high up in trees, snap insects out of the air, or snatch fishes from waters far out at sea. Many birds eat several kinds of food. Plant-eating birds, for example, feed on seeds, fruit, or nectar. When insects are plentiful, these birds may eat them, too.

Like insects, birds help plants reproduce. When a bird eats seeds or fruits, many of the seeds pass through the bird's body intact. Hours or days later, the bird will release these seeds in its droppings. Some of the seeds may fall on fertile soil, take root, and grow into new plants. Birds also help plants by eating insects that destroy leaves, roots, or bark.

Birds hunt most kinds of animals: plankton animals, hydras, jellyfishes, mollusks, worms, insects, crusta-ceans, arachnids, echinoderms, fishes, amphibians, and reptiles. Some birds also hunt other birds and mammals. Scavenger birds eat dead animals.

Beaks and Feet

Each bird has a beak, which helps it get the kinds of food it wants to eat. Beaks are strong yet light. By growing all the time, beaks never wear out. Some beaks are long and sharp for spearing fishes. Others are short and stout for cracking seeds. The limpkin's long, slender beak probes the mud for worms, and an eagle's hooked beak tears into animal flesh. A wood-pecker's chisel-like beak picks out insects hidden un-der tree bark. A duck's beak strains tiny plants and animals from the water. And a hummingbird's long beak probes inside flowers for sweet nectar.

Like all animals, birds need water. Many birds get their water from the food they eat. Others drink dew off plants or fresh water from puddles, rivers, and lakes. Seabirds have special glands near their nostrils that get rid of harmful salt in the seawater.

Nearly all birds have scales covering their legs and feet. These are the only scales on a bird's body, and they are similar to reptile scales.

Wild turkeys eat berries.

GROUND BIRDS Some birds, such as turkeys, quails, pheasants, and prairie chickens, spend much of their lives on the ground. Most of these ground birds can run rapidly and their short, round wings let them fly fast for short distances. Using their strong, clawed feet, ground birds often scratch the soil for seeds, berries, and insects to eat.

The snowy ptarmigan grows white feathers in winter and dark brown ones in summer.

Rather than fly, a brilliantly colored golden pheasant runs from danger.

Male prairie chickens gather to dance before females.

A Victoria crowned pigeon can grow to be 29 inches (73 cm) long.

Suddenly a bob-white flies from its hiding place.

With their legs and feet, birds land, climb, run, scratch the ground, swim, walk, and defend themselves. Some birds, especially birds of prey, use the sharp claws on their powerful feet to seize and kill other animals. Wading birds have feet with long, straight toes. And swimming birds usually have webbed feet, which help them paddle along in the water or walk on mud without sinking.

Perching birds, such as robins, sparrows, and warblers, have four toes on each foot. Three point forward and one points backward. Perching birds rest and sleep in trees or bushes. When they bend their legs, their toes curl around a branch and tightly lock into place so that the birds don't fall off.

Some birds sleep with their beaks tucked under their wings. During the night they fluff their feathers to keep warm. Often, hundreds of the same kind of bird fly to a tree to roost together.

Birds recognize other birds by their colors, patterns, and calls. Calls are especially important during the breeding season.

To get the attention of a peahen, an Indian peacock raises his fantail and shakes it.

TROPICAL BIRDS In a tropical rain forest live many brightly colored birds. They feed on insects, fruits, and nuts. Parrots and other tropical birds often scream to one another.

Before eating a bee, the bee-eater removes the stinger.

At the end of the mating season, the male quetzal will shed his very long tail feathers.

The male great hornbill helps wall the female and her eggs into a tree hole. Then he feeds her through a slit in the wall.

The largest parrot, the scarlet macaw, cracks open hard nuts with its beak.

Breeding Season

At the start of the breeding season, a male bird often claims a territory that has plenty of food and a safe place to build a nest. Then he announces his claim by calling out to other males of his species. His call tells them to leave at once and stay away. Should another male ignore his warning, he will defend the territory with his beak, wings, and claws.

From inside his territory, a male bird also calls out to attract a female. His call announces that he would like to mate. Different birds sing, honk, quack, whistle, hoot, caw, or click when they call. Female birds listen for the calls of their own species. Just a few species of female birds sing along with the males.

Calls are only one signal a male and female bird give to each other. Once a female enters a male's territory, other signals may have to be given before the two can mate. During courtship, birds may dance, strut, coo, shake their heads, touch beaks, or bow. They may perform daring acrobatics in midair, scream, or show off by displaying dazzling feathers.

Hovering in the air, a red-tailed comet h u m m i n g b i r d plunges its long beak into a trumpet flower in search of nectar.

The rainbow toucan's large, brightly colored beak plucks a fruit to eat.

PERCHING BIRDS More than 5,000 of the 8,600 species of birds are perching birds. Among them are songbirds such as nightingales, larks, thrushes, and warblers.

A house sparrow takes a dust bath.

canopy

Each year, social weaverbirds add new nests onto the large canopy they built together.

cowbird egg

Cliff swallows build their mud nests side by side.

Inside its egg, a robin is nearly ready to hatch.

This brown-headed cowbird lives in the United States. Like some cuckoo birds, it lays its egg in another bird's nest. The other bird parents raise the baby cowbird.

Long-tailed antbirds follow army ants. These birds eat the insects, frogs, and lizards that flee from the approaching ant army.

After pulling small clumps of fur off a woodchuck's back, a tufted titmouse lines its nest with the fur.

This blue jay is anting. It has opened its wings so that ants can eat feather lice.

80

Male birds are usually the most colorful during breeding season. Females are attracted to the male's bright-colored feathers. Bright feathers also serve as a warning to other males to stay away—or else.

Female birds rarely have bright-colored feathers. Instead, their feathers have colors that help female birds hide on the ground, in trees, or in their nests. After breeding season is over, many male birds lose their bright feathers and grow a set that helps conceal them, too.

Nests and Eggs

Birds build their nests in safe places that are protected from the hot sun and cold rain. In some species, both parents build their nest together. In others, either the male or the female builds alone.

Birds are not taught how to build their nests. By instinct, they know how to do it. Different birds build their nests in trees, in bushes, in tall grass, on water, in caves, on rocky island cliffs, in tree trunks, in burrows, or on the ground.

Most birds build cup-shaped nests made of twigs, leaves, grass, or weeds. Others build their nests of moss and cobwebs or stones and mud. Different birds build nests with domes, nests with chambers inside, hanging purse-shaped nests, tube-shaped nests, even nests in between leaves the birds sew together. Each nest has to be strong enough to hold eggs and to resist being blown away by the wind. To help keep their eggs warm, birds often line their nests with feathers, bark, mud, moss, or mammal hairs.

Soon after mating, a female bird lays her eggs. Although some ducks can lay 20 eggs at one time, most birds lay fewer than six.

Unlike most other animals, birds protect and take care of their eggs and young. While one parent sits on the eggs to conceal them and keep them warm, the other hunts and returns with food.

A baby bird develops inside each fertilized egg. The yellow egg yolk supplies it with food. Around the yolk is the egg white, or albumen. It protects the developing bird and keeps it from drying out. Tiny pores in the hard eggshell let in oxygen and let out some wastes. If an egg gets cold, the baby bird dies.

When a bird is ready to hatch, it grows a hard egg tooth on its beak. With this tooth, it scrapes at the shell until the shell breaks. Shortly after hatching, the egg tooth drops off.

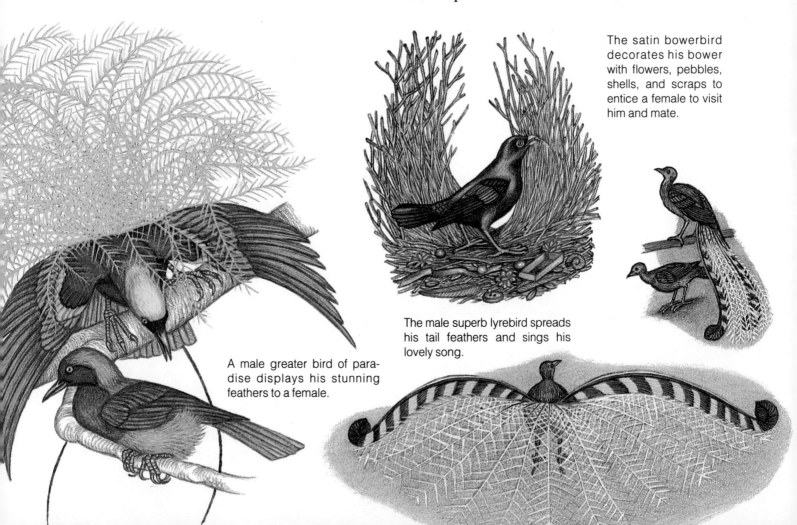

The satin bowerbird decorates his bower with flowers, pebbles, shells, and scraps to entice a female to visit him and mate.

A male greater bird of paradise displays his stunning feathers to a female.

The male superb lyrebird spreads his tail feathers and sings his lovely song.

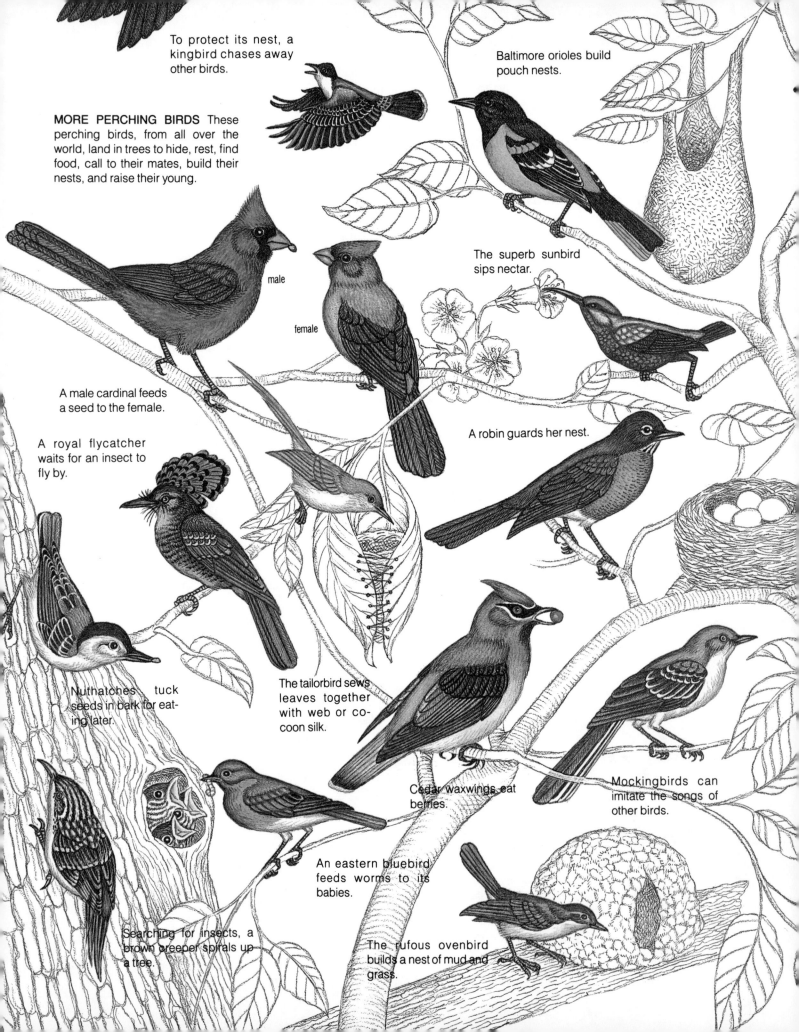

To protect its nest, a kingbird chases away other birds.

MORE PERCHING BIRDS These perching birds, from all over the world, land in trees to hide, rest, find food, call to their mates, build their nests, and raise their young.

Baltimore orioles build pouch nests.

male

female

A male cardinal feeds a seed to the female.

The superb sunbird sips nectar.

A royal flycatcher waits for an insect to fly by.

A robin guards her nest.

Nuthatches tuck seeds in bark for eating later.

The tailorbird sews leaves together with web or cocoon silk.

Mockingbirds can imitate the songs of other birds.

Cedar waxwings eat berries.

An eastern bluebird feeds worms to its babies.

Searching for insects, a brown creeper spirals up a tree.

The rufous ovenbird builds a nest of mud and grass.

BLACKPOLL WARBLER

BLACK-THROATED BLUE WARBLER

Three migrating warblers rest.

YELLOW WARBLER

A penduline tit weaves its nest around a branch.

A woodpecker finch uses a thorn to get at insects hiding under bark.

Long-tailed grass finches help each other preen.

In winter the male scarlet tanager is greenish yellow. In spring he is red and black.

At the edge of the woods, a meadowlark sings.

To claim his territory, a red-winged blackbird calls out and shows his bright wing patches.

Growing Up

Some baby birds, such as ducklings, hatch with their eyes open and their bodies covered with soft down feathers. Because they can find food, their parents don't have to bring it to them. Even though ducklings can swim almost immediately, their mother protects them and helps keep them warm at night. When a predator is near, a duck will call out in alarm to warn its ducklings. If a duckling gets lost, it calls out in distress.

Most baby birds hatch from their eggs featherless, blind, and helpless. They have to be fed, kept warm, and protected all the time. It takes a few days for them to grow down feathers and for their eyes to open. Only after a few weeks in the nest are these birds ready to fly and find their own food. In the meantime, they keep their parents busy feeding them, fluffing the nest lining, and cleaning the nest.

Baby birds beg for food all the time. They call out or peck at their parents to let them know how hungry they are. Begging makes the parents fly off in search of more food. Some birds make 30 trips an hour, from morning to night, to gather enough food.

When the parents return to their nest with food, they have to be very careful not to lead other animals to it. If a hungry squirrel, snake, monkey, or raccoon discovers the nest, the parents may have to attack the predator in order to save their young. Some gulls, crows, and birds of prey raid the nests of other birds.

Many birds swallow food for their young and store it in their crop (page 70). When they land on the nest, their babies call out, peck at them, or with beaks wide open show off bright-colored mouth spots. Calls, pecks, and colors make the parents cough up the half-digested seeds, berries, worms, or fishes in their crop. At times, there isn't enough food for all the babies. Then the strongest, largest babies are best able to compete for what food there is. The weaker ones can't get enough and die.

With constant feeding, baby birds grow quickly. Before they leave the nest, their parents often teach them how to fly and find food. Finally the young birds are off on their own, adding their graceful movements, flashing colors, and beautiful sounds to those of the billions of birds in the animal world.

83

backbone

skull

ribs   foal

hoof

INSIDE A MUSTANG A horse's skeleton supports and protects its delicate body parts. Like all mammals, horses breathe air into their lungs, make heat inside their bodies, and grow hair. The foal developing inside this female horse is almost ready to be born. Female mammals produce milk to feed their babies.

baby

After hatching from its egg, a baby echidna feeds on the milk oozing from its mother's belly skin. Echidnas and the duck-billed platypuses are the only egg-laying mammals.

ECHIDNA

eggs

Mammals

DOGS, CATS, RABBITS, cows, pigs, horses, lions, and tigers are bony animals called mammals. The largest land and sea animals are mammals. So, too, are the most intelligent animals in the animal world.

The 4,200 species of mammals live nearly everywhere. Polar bears roam the frigid Arctic, camels stride across hot desert sands, monkeys climb to the tops of tall trees, whales dive deep in ocean waters, bats fly from their caves, moles burrow underground, herds of elephants tramp through forests, mountain goats scale steep slopes, and zebras graze on flat grasslands.

Mammals are the only hairy animals. They are also the only animals that make milk for their babies. All mammals, even those living in the sea, breathe air into their lungs.

Fur, whiskers, and wool are different kinds of mammal hair. Hair protects a mammal's skin. It is sensitive to touch and helps prevent necessary body heat from escaping. Most mammals grow lots of hairs. Others, such as walruses, grow just a few short hairs on their faces. Still others grow hair only before they are born.

Like birds, mammals make their own heat and so are able to keep their bodies warm night and day, all year long. For this reason most mammals can be active at night or in cold weather. If a mammal overheats, it can stretch out its body to let heat escape or pant with its tongue hanging out. Most mammals can also sweat to help cool down. Mammals are the only animals with sweat glands in their skin.

Baby mammals feed on their mother's milk. Milk is an excellent food, containing water, proteins, sugar, fats, vitamins, and minerals. It is produced by special skin glands, called mammary glands, which only mammals have.

EGG-LAYING MAMMALS

Echidnas and duck-billed platypuses are the only mammals that lay eggs. Their eggs have leathery shells like the eggs of reptiles.

While this male duck-billed platypus swims, the female, in her burrow, curls around her eggs to keep them warm and safe until they hatch.

POUCHED MAMMALS

Baby kangaroos and baby opossums start life as fertilized eggs growing inside their mother's body. After only a few days, they are born blind, hairless, and helpless. To stay alive, each baby has to crawl into its mother's safe, warm pouch, find a nipple, and start feeding on milk. In the pouch, development is slowly completed. There are about 250 species of marsupials, or pouched mammals, and most live in Australia.

To protect her young, an opossum may hiss and show her teeth. Opossums live in the Americas.

At night the Tasmanian devil hunts birds, lizards, and small mammals.

Koalas eat eucalyptus leaves.

Returning inside its mother's pouch, this baby large gray kangaroo, or joey (**left**), is safe from danger. Using its tail for balance, the ring-tailed rock wallaby (**right**) can jump 12 feet (3.6 m).

A bandicoot's pouch opens to the rear.

After spending the day hidden in their deep burrow, a wombat and her baby come out to search for plants to eat.

85

All other kinds of baby mammals grow inside their mother's body until they are ready to be born. Baby mice develop inside for 20 days, whereas baby elephants need 20 months.

Inside its mother, a baby mammal is well protected and kept at the right temperature by her warm body. Each baby develops from a fertilized egg cell that has no shell and very little food. By a special attachment to its mother, called a placenta, each baby gets all the food and oxygen it needs from its mother's blood.

Most mammals have only a few babies. Mice, for example, can give birth to six or seven babies at one time. Newborn mice are blind, helpless, and hairless. They drink milk from nipples on their mother's belly.

Whales, monkeys, elephants, and horses usually have only one baby at a time. A baby horse not only can see and hear when it is born but also can run around within hours. Even so, it still needs milk.

Baby mammals get a lot of care from their mothers (and sometimes from their fathers, too). They are fed, protected, and licked clean. Many mammals build nests or dens where they care for their families. During the care period, a close bond can develop between a mammal and its young.

Gradually, baby mammals start eating solid food. When they are fully weaned, they no longer need milk. Until they can take care of themselves, their parents continue to care for them. From their parents, most baby mammals learn how to find food, defend themselves, and avoid danger.

INSECT EATERS

All the mammals illustrated on these two pages eat insects. Some also eat worms, snails, frogs, or tender plant parts. Except for anteaters and pangolins, all of them have teeth.

Using their massive claws, armadillos, aardvarks, anteaters, and pangolins rip into ant and termite nests to get at the insects living inside. And whereas small shrews search the forest floor for food, most moles spend almost their entire lives in underground tunnels they dig with their shovel-like front feet.

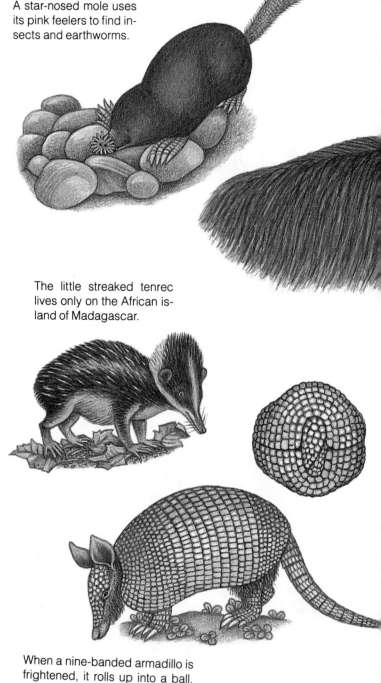

A star-nosed mole uses its pink feelers to find insects and earthworms.

The little streaked tenrec lives only on the African island of Madagascar.

When a nine-banded armadillo is frightened, it rolls up into a ball, protected by its tough skin.

Baby white-toothed shrews follow in a line behind their mother.

With its powerful claws, a giant anteater rips into a termite mound to find food. The anteater is 3.3 feet (1 m) long.

INSECT-EATING MAMMALS

The tree pangolin's "scales" are made of special hairs stuck together.

A pink fairy armadillo grows to be only 6 inches (15 cm) long.

An aardvark uses its long, sticky tongue to trap insects.

Sharp spines protect the spiny hedgehog's body.

The Russian desman's flat tail and webbed feet help it swim.

Only rarely does this blind golden mole leave its underground tunnels and come to the surface.

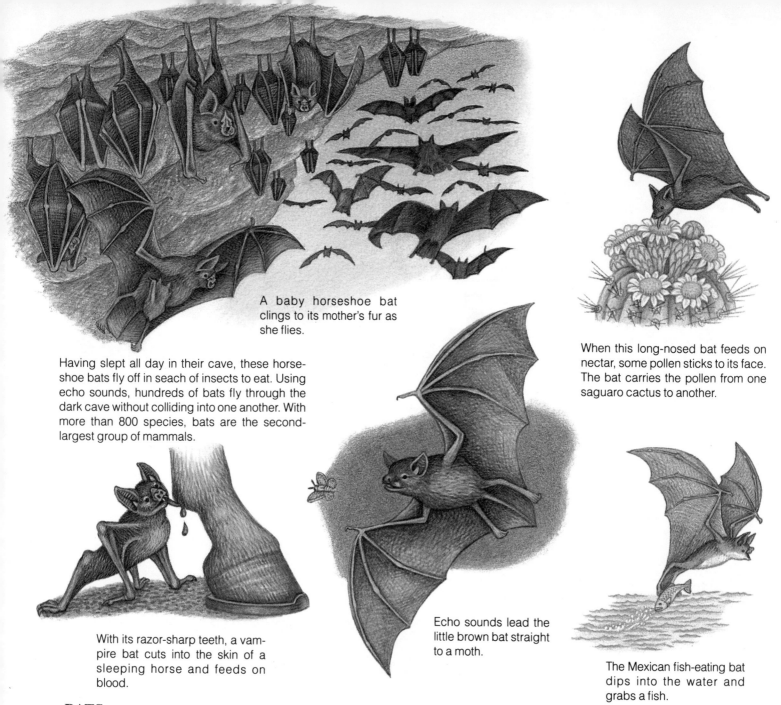

A baby horseshoe bat clings to its mother's fur as she flies.

Having slept all day in their cave, these horseshoe bats fly off in seach of insects to eat. Using echo sounds, hundreds of bats fly through the dark cave without colliding into one another. With more than 800 species, bats are the second-largest group of mammals.

When this long-nosed bat feeds on nectar, some pollen sticks to its face. The bat carries the pollen from one saguaro cactus to another.

With its razor-sharp teeth, a vampire bat cuts into the skin of a sleeping horse and feeds on blood.

Echo sounds lead the little brown bat straight to a moth.

The Mexican fish-eating bat dips into the water and grabs a fish.

BATS

Bats are the only mammals able to fly. Their wings are made of thin, hairless, elastic skin that stretches between their long fingers. Each wing runs along the side of a bat's body down to its tail.

Most bats are night hunters. When they fly, they send out high-pitched sounds from their nose or mouth. If these sounds hit an object, such as a flying insect, they bounce off and echo back to the bat's ears. From the returning echoes, the bat can tell exactly where the insect is. Bats fly so well that they can catch insects in midair. As they fly in darkness, bats also use echoes to avoid crashing into rocks, trees, and other bats.

Not all bats eat just insects. Some hunt fishes, frogs, mice, lizards, or even other kinds of bats. Fruit-eating bats search for ripe fruits, and vampire bats lap up blood oozing out of wounds they make in the bodies of other animals.

During the day most bats sleep hanging upside down in caves. When a bat sleeps, its body temperature drops, saving energy. On awakening, a bat has to exercise its muscles before it can fly. Many bats hibernate through winter in their caves. Rarely do they wake up before spring returns.

RODENTS

Nearly one half of all mammals are rodents. This group includes squirrels, beavers, rats, and mice. Rodents use their chisel-like front teeth to gnaw at nuts, grains, bark, roots, and other plant parts. These gnawing teeth, which grow all the time, are constantly worn down and sharpened by the foods rodents eat. Rodents also eat insects and worms.

Some rodents have cheek pouches, in which they store food to carry back to their underground burrows or dens. In their homes, rodents raise their young, store food, sleep, and hide from the birds, reptiles, and large mammals that hunt them. Many rodents also spend part or all of the winter hibernating in the safety of their homes.

Flying squirrels glide by spreading their skin flaps like parachutes.

A dormouse can sleep six to eight months during cold weather.

This chipmunk has filled its cheek pouches with seeds it will store in its burrow.

Long-legged maras, which live in Argentina, can run at 18 miles per hour (28 kph).

With their sharp teeth, beavers gnaw down trees to get branches for building. First they build a dam to make a pond. On the pond, each beaver family builds a lodge to live in. Hidden underwater are tunnels in and out of the lodge.

am

lodge

tunnel

MORE RODENTS Rodents live all over the world. They eat plant parts such as bark, roots, and tough grass as well as insects and worms. Rodents make up the largest group of mammals.

JAGUAR

To escape a jaguar (a carnivore), this capybara hides in the water.

Pacas come out at night to look for food.

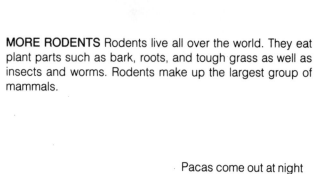

The white-throated wood rat collects shiny things to take back to its nest.

To let males know she is ready to mate, this golden hamster leaves her scent on rocks and sticks. Other mammals do this too.

BEAR CUB

Desert kangaroo rats seldom drink. They get all their water from the seeds they eat.

The porcupine's sharp quills wound an overly curious bear cub (a carnivore) that has come too near.

Pocket gophers fill their cheek pouches with roots to eat.

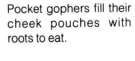

When there isn't enough food, Norway lemmings migrate in search of something to eat.

Chinchillas live high up in the mountains of Bolivia and Chile.

An Old World harvest mouse weaves a nest of grass for her young.

Baby voles hang on to their mother's nipples.

Prairie dogs live together in underground towns. Out in the open they feed and play, always watching for intruders. At the first sign of danger one prairie dog will signal the others to quickly return to safety underground. When prairie dogs greet each other, they touch noses. This helps them recognize the prairie dogs that live in their town. Others are not welcome.

In tree holes, red squirrels store food for winter.

BURROWING OWL

SOME LARGE AND SMALL MAMMALS

Except for sloths, none of the mammals illustrated here are closely related to other mammals. For this reason, they are in their own groups: gliding lemurs; rabbits, hares, and pikas; elephants; tree shrews; and hyraxes. Sloths are related to anteaters and armadillos (pages 86–87).

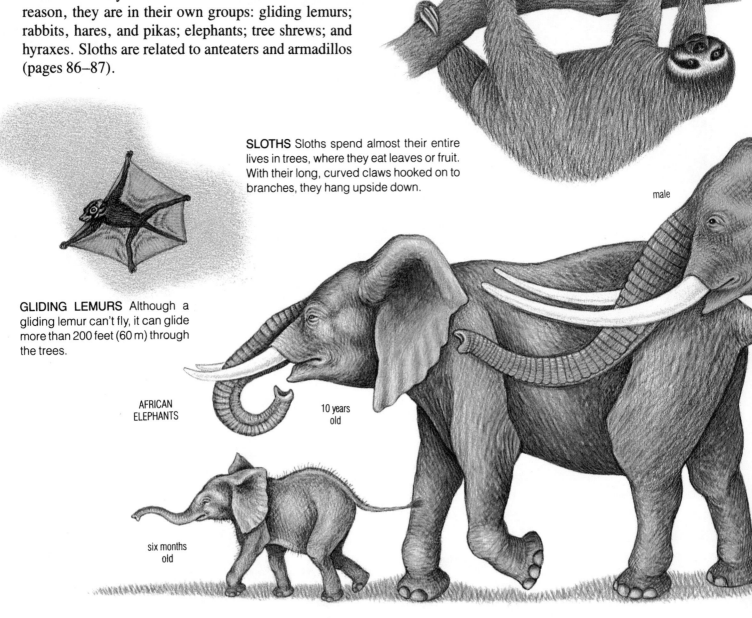

THREE-TOED SLOTH

SLOTHS Sloths spend almost their entire lives in trees, where they eat leaves or fruit. With their long, curved claws hooked on to branches, they hang upside down.

male

GLIDING LEMURS Although a gliding lemur can't fly, it can glide more than 200 feet (60 m) through the trees.

AFRICAN ELEPHANTS

10 years old

six months old

ELEPHANTS Elephants are the largest, most powerful land animals. Some stand more than 12 feet (3.6 m) high and weigh over 12,000 pounds (5,400 kg). There are only two species, the African and the Indian elephant. Indian elephants are smaller than African elephants. Elephants use their strong, flexible trunks for smelling and touching. With their trunks, they also lift food and water to their mouths. Elephants may spend more than 16 hours a day searching for food. One adult elephant may eat more than 500 pounds (225 kg) of plants a day and drink 40 gallons (180 liters) of water. An elephant's ivory tusks are really long, curved teeth, which can be used as weapons or to peel bark from trees.

a

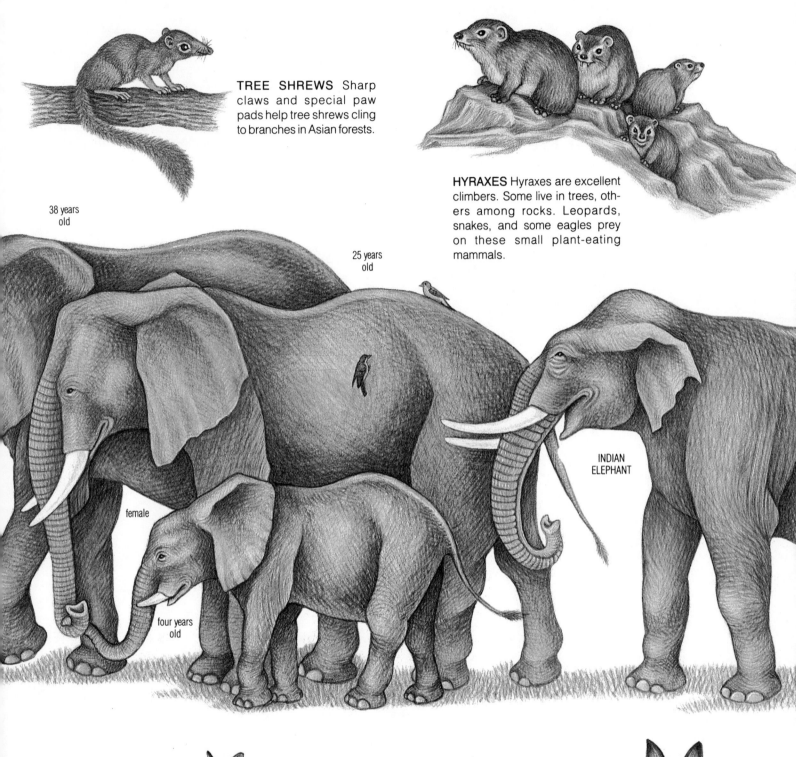

TREE SHREWS Sharp claws and special paw pads help tree shrews cling to branches in Asian forests.

HYRAXES Hyraxes are excellent climbers. Some live in trees, others among rocks. Leopards, snakes, and some eagles prey on these small plant-eating mammals.

38 years old

25 years old

female

four years old

INDIAN ELEPHANT

RABBITS, HARES, AND PIKAS Like rodents, rabbits and hares have gnawing teeth. Rabbits live in burrows, but hares hide among plants. Rabbits are born blind and helpless, but hares are born with their eyes open and with fur on their bodies. In late summer, pikas (**a**) gather grass and plant stems, dry them in the sun, and store them under rocks as food for winter. When it senses danger, one European rabbit (**b**) stomps its feet, a signal for the others to run to safety in their burrows. With its long ears, a jackrabbit (**c**) listens for a nearby predator. Jackrabbits are hares.

b

c

93

SEA MAMMALS

The giants of the sea aren't fishes, but whales. Whales, manatees, and dugongs are sea mammals that live their entire lives in the water. Seals, walruses, and sea lions also live in the sea, but they come on land to sun and raise their families.

Nearly all sea mammals have a thick layer of fat, called blubber, under their skin. Blubber helps sea mammals keep warm in cold waters. Sea mammals also have flippers instead of feet. Whereas whales have only a pair of front flippers, seals, walruses, and sea lions have both front and rear flippers.

Sea mammals usually move about in search of food. Toothless whales filter out plankton and other small animals from seawater. Toothed whales, including dolphins, porpoises, and sperm and white whales,

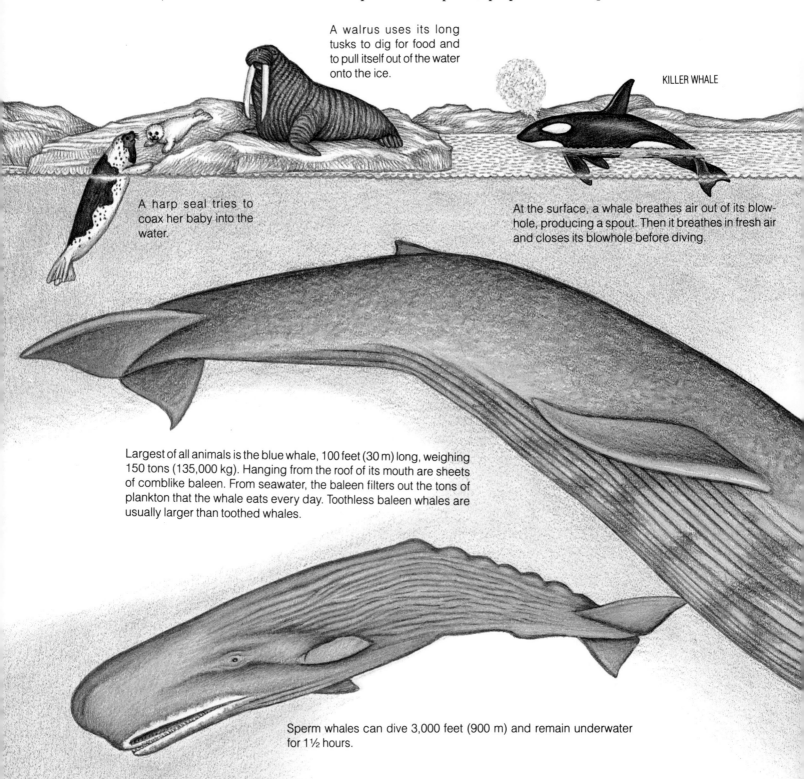

A walrus uses its long tusks to dig for food and to pull itself out of the water onto the ice.

KILLER WHALE

A harp seal tries to coax her baby into the water.

At the surface, a whale breathes air out of its blow-hole, producing a spout. Then it breathes in fresh air and closes its blowhole before diving.

Largest of all animals is the blue whale, 100 feet (30 m) long, weighing 150 tons (135,000 kg). Hanging from the roof of its mouth are sheets of comblike baleen. From seawater, the baleen filters out the tons of plankton that the whale eats every day. Toothless baleen whales are usually larger than toothed whales.

Sperm whales can dive 3,000 feet (900 m) and remain underwater for 1½ hours.

hunt squids, mackerels, herrings, cuttlefishes, seals, and sharks.

Whales often live and travel in groups. Few other animals attack them because they are so gigantic. Some whales migrate thousands of miles from cool polar waters to warmer seas, where they breed. Humpback whales perform complicated songs for hours at a time.

During breeding season, sea lions live in colonies on rocks.

Two huge male elephant seals fight for territory before the females arrive to mate.

A humpback whale breaches by leaping out of the water.

PENGUIN

LEOPARD SEAL

Although it is shown here in cold waters, a manatee lives in warm coastal waters, eating plants.

Like bats, toothed whales, such as this dolphin, use echoes to find food. Echoes also help them avoid underwater collisions.

A killer whale chases a leopard seal hunting a penguin.

This baby white whale is feeding on its mother's milk.

baleen

plankton

Male narwhals have one tooth that grows into a long tusk.

A raccoon spends most of the day resting before it hunts at night.

At the river's edge a huge Alaskan brown bear, 8 feet (2.4 m) tall, catches a salmon.

Suddenly a red fox pounces on a mouse.

In the swamp grass, a maned wolf stalks a paca (page 90).

High up in Asian mountains, red pandas live in trees.

Even though the giant panda is a carnivore, it eats mainly bamboo shoots and leaves.

CARNIVORES

On land, the fiercest hunters are the mammals called carnivores. Lions, tigers, wolves, and weasels are just some of these cunning animals. Nearly all carnivores hunt other mammals, birds, or fishes. Some, such as bears and raccoons, also eat plants and honey.

Alert and active, carnivores are armed with strong jaws, sharp claws, muscular legs, and quick reflexes. Their pointed front teeth stab and hold their prey, their slicing teeth rip into flesh, and their sharp cheek teeth crack and chop bones.

Most carnivores hunt alone. But some, such as lions, hyenas, and wolves, hunt together in groups. By sniffing, carnivores pick up animal scents stuck to plants or carried by the wind. Silently, they stalk their prey, often hiding among rocks or plants where their colors blend in so well that the carnivores seem to disappear. To avoid alerting their prey, nearly all carnivores will wait as long as they have to without moving. By turning their ears in different directions, they pick up sounds all around them.

The nearer carnivores get to their prey, the more they rely on their vision to help them figure out how safe it is to attack. When they are ready, they move in slowly. Then, at just the right moment, they pounce, grasping with their sharp claws and biting, or they break into a fast run to catch or corner their prey. Frequently the prey escapes, but hungry carnivores keep hunting.

Many carnivores hunt large, plant-eating mammals such as antelopes, zebras, and buffaloes that travel in herds. Instead of attacking the entire herd, carnivores

Sometimes an Arctic fox trails polar bears. The fox hopes to find food scraps left over after the bears eat a seal.

A coyote howls on the prairie.

A pack of gray wolves follows tracks in the snow. The strongest wolves, with their tails raised, lead the pack. Other wolves, with their tails lowered, obey them.

MORE CARNIVORES

Curious, playful river otters slide down mud hills into the water.

The honey guide bird leads the honey badger to a beehive. After the badger claws open the hive and eats some honey, the bird feeds on the honey that remains, wax, and larvas.

To make climbing easier, the binturong wraps its tail around branches.

The African palm civet climbs a tree to eat a fruit.

A least weasel, 7 inches (18 cm) long, snarls at a fisher, 3.3 feet (1 m) long, trying to scare it away. Both animals are carnivores.

learn to select and attack a weak animal or one that has strayed from the others.

Hunting antelopes, zebras, or buffaloes is hard work, for these grazing animals are powerful and fast and have hooves, horns, and teeth to defend themselves. Carnivores must outwit their prey and avoid injury to themselves while they make their kill.

Once carnivores make a kill, they may guard it so that other animals can't eat it. The parts they don't eat immediately they cover with leaves, bury, or drag up a tree to be eaten later. After carnivores have finished eating, scraps often remain for jackals, hyenas, vultures, and rats.

Like many other mammals, carnivores often claim territories where they live and hunt. To mark off their claims, they leave scents on bushes or rocks or scratch

If this wolverine doesn't back away, the striped skunk will spray it with a foul-smelling fluid. Both animals are carnivores.

A crow tries to prevent a pine marten from stealing her eggs.

This black-footed ferret has taken over a prairie dog burrow as home for her family.

On the island of Madagascar, fossas hunt for small mammals, birds, and lizards.

The western polecat marks his territory with a scent he produces.

The sea otter is a carnivore that lives most of its life at sea. It sleeps wrapped in seaweed so that it won't drift away.

claw marks on trees. In this way, they let other animals of their own species know the territory is taken. Each carnivore explores its territory to learn where the best hunting is and where there is water. In their territories, carnivores build lairs, dens, or burrows for resting and hiding.

In winter, bears, raccoons, and badgers retire to their dens and fall into a light sleep. Their bodies stay warm enough for them to wake up often and move around before falling asleep again. During this period, female bears give birth to their cubs and nurse them.

In breeding season, male and female carnivores follow each other's scents. Before mating, they sometimes touch, kiss, wrestle, or play. Carnivore babies are born helpless. As they grow, they learn from their parents how to be expert hunters.

99

Tigers are the largest cats. They live alone, hunting deer, cattle, and wild pigs. This Bengal tiger, 9 feet (2.7 m) long, has come out of the tall grass, where its stripes and colors helped keep it well hidden.

Except for cheetahs, cats can retract (pull in) their claws so that they don't get damaged. This Pallas's cat lives in Central Asia.

An ocelot yowls to scare away a predator.

At 70 miles per hour (112 kph), the cheetah can run faster than any other animal.

A house cat plays with yarn.

When they are a few months old, snow leopards learn from their mother how to hunt.

CATS Armed with strong muscles, sharp claws and teeth, keen senses, soft paws for moving quietly, and sensitive whiskers, cats are among the most skillful hunters in the animal world. All cats are carnivores.

In her den, a mountain lion cares for her cubs. Mountain lions are also known as cougars or pumas.

In search of prey, a jaguar patrols his territory. Jaguars live in the United States and Central and South America.

With its long, tufted ears, forward-looking eyes, powerful muscles, and long, sharp claws, the caracal sits ready to defend itself.

Having stalked a snowshoe hare, a bobcat quickly moves in to make its kill.

An African lion roars to drive away another lion trying to take over his territory. While his females hunt, the African lion rests. After a kill is made by the females, he gets to eat first.

It is dusk on the African plain. A leopard has killed a gazelle and carried it up into a tree to eat later. Vultures pick away at the remains of a zebra killed by female lions. While birds eat ticks living on a black rhinoceros's skin, a topi stands on a termite mound to look around. Alarmed warthogs run, impalas leap from hunting dogs, and a spotted hyena watches some nearby gazelles. When carnivores have full stomachs, plant-eating hoofed mammals are in the least danger.

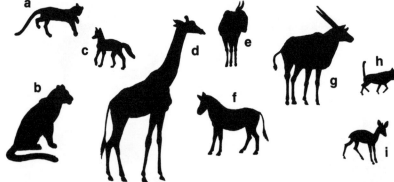

HOOFED MAMMALS

On the African plains live many of the big, long-legged plant-eating mammals hunted by carnivores. Very large herds of buffaloes, zebras, and wildebeests graze on plains grass while elands nibble at shrubs, antelopes browse in low bushes, and giraffes reach high up in trees to nip off leaves and buds. Most of these plant eaters walk and run on the hooves covering the tips of their toes.

No matter where hoofed mammals feed, they are usually in danger. Because they are so big, they are easy to spot from a distance. As they move, their bodies give off scents that stick to plants or are carried by the wind, creating a trail that hungry carnivores can follow.

VULTUF

CARNIVORES: (a) leopard, (b) lion, (c) black-backed jackal, (m) spotted hyena, and (q) African hunting dog.

HOOFED MAMMALS: (d) giraffe, (e) white-bearded gnu, (f) zebra, (g) eland, (h) warthog, (i) dik-dik, (j) black rhinoceros, (k) Thomson's gazelle, (l) topi, (n) cape buffalo, (o) impala, and (p) waterbuck.

Often, hoofed mammals feed in the open, where it is most difficult for carnivores to sneak up on them unseen. They constantly listen for sounds or sniff for the smell of a hungry lion or cheetah lurking nearby. Even with their heads down, they see in all directions with their large eyes, alert to any suspicious movements.

If one animal in a herd suddenly puts its head up high and stares or starts running, or if a bird cries, the other hoofed mammals heed the alarm. Some stampede, causing confusion as they try to outrun a predator. Others flee for cover in tall grasses or among bushes and rocks, where their colors make them hard to find. Wherever they hide, they must stand still, for the slightest movement may give them away. If a predator gets too near, they may spring from hiding so unexpectedly that the surprise allows time for escape.

While hoofed mammals seem gentle and harmless when they feed, they fiercely defend themselves and their families if threatened. Their blunt hooves can

HOOVES Many mammals walk on their hoofed toes. The bongo walks on two toes of each foot. Like it, pigs, sheep, goats, deer, antelopes, cattle, and hippopotamuses have an even number of hoofed toes on each foot.

Horses have just one hoofed toe on each foot. Other odd-toed hoofed mammals are zebras, tapirs, and rhinoceroses.

BONGO

PRZEWALSKI HORSE

MOUNTAIN GOAT

Vicunas and mountain goats climb high in the mountains. They have special toe pads that do not slip easily on rocks.

toe pad

VICUNA

sheath

PRONGHORN
ANTELOPE

BIGHORN
SHEEP

b

SABLE
ANTELOPE

c

GREATER
KUDU

HORNS Okapis and giraffes grow short horns made of bone covered by skin and hair. The pronghorn's horns are made of bone covered by a sheath. Every year the sheath falls off and a new one grows in its place. Sheep (**a**), antelopes (**b**, **c**), cattle (**d**), and goats have bony horns covered by a sheath, but their sheath never falls off. As their permanent horns grow, they may curve or twist.

OKAPI

d

MUSK OX

This moose, 10 feet (3 m) high, is the largest deer.

ANTLERS Deer don't grow horns. Instead, nearly all male deer grow solid, bony antlers. Each year, after mating season, their antlers fall off (**a**). Then the deer grow new antlers (**b**), which get larger and may branch (**c**). During antler growth, the antlers are covered with a soft skin, called velvet. Later the velvet peels off. Female reindeer and caribou also grow antlers.

MOOSE

a

velvet

b

c

MULE
DEER

105

strike fatal blows at any attacker. Many hoofed mammals also grow tusks, horns, or antlers, some of the deadliest weapons in the animal world.

As they feed, most hoofed mammals swallow their food without chewing it completely. Later, when they are resting in a safe place, the partially digested food, or cud, returns to their mouth a little at a time to be rechewed completely before it is reswallowed.

When there are lots of plants to eat, herds of hoofed mammals grow larger and larger. If they grew too

Once, millions of bison grazed the North American plains. Today there are only a few thousand.

The small chevrotain, 20 inches (50 cm) long, feeds at night on grass and leaves.

In a forest clearing, two large male elks (**a**) fight over a group of female does (**b**). When one male backs down and flees, the other can mate with the does. Nearby, a white-tailed deer (**c**) licks her fawn, hidden in the grass. Since fawns are born without a scent, they are difficult for predators to find. Away from the elks, a baby caribou (**d**), born a few hours earlier, follows its mother.

large, there would be so many animals eating plants that the plants would be destroyed. By constantly hunting plant eaters, carnivores keep the numbers in the herds down. Carnivores also keep the herds moving so that they never stay in one place long enough to destroy the plants on which they depend.

Most of the meat that human beings eat comes from hoofed mammals. People have domesticated (raised and tamed) cattle, sheep, pigs, and horses for food or to do work.

As a young tapir grows, it loses its stripes and spots.

Camels don't store water in their humps; they store fat for energy. Dromedary camels have one hump; bactrian camels (**a**) have two. A camel can go for six to eight days without drinking. When it finds water, though, a thirsty camel might drink more than 20 gallons (90 l) in a few minutes. The addax (**b**), oryx (**c**), somali ass (**d**), and gerenuk (**e**) are also hoofed mammals that live in the desert.

While a hippopotamus cools off in the water, her baby swims.

PRIMATES

As it swings through the trees a gibbon suddenly sees a bird fly by. In a split second, the gibbon judges how far away the bird is and grabs it. Returning to his family, the gibbon shares his catch with them.

Gibbons are apes. Apes, monkeys, lemurs, and tarsiers are part of the group of mammals called primates.

Most primates live in trees and eat fruits, leaves, or insects. By wrapping their five fingers or toes around branches, they cling tightly as they climb or hang.

With their forward-looking eyes and sharp vision, primates can accurately judge how far to leap or move to grab food without falling.

Primates are usually peaceful animals. Even ferocious-looking apes keep to themselves and rarely bother any other animal.

Many primates live together in groups. In a group of gorillas, the most powerful male rules as leader. Among chimpanzees, many males may help lead a group.

Chimpanzees are very intelligent, clever animals. They are able to use sticks as tools. To communicate

It's morning in the jungle. Monkeys, apes, and lemurs are waking while other primates are ready to sleep. Primates are mammals. Most live in trees, although some monkeys and apes live on the ground. Monkeys have tails; apes do not. Instead of claws or hooves, nearly all primates have fingernails and toenails. Although they are shown here together, not all of these primates live in the same place. (a) Suction pads on its fingers and toes help the Philippine tarsier cling to trees. (b) Howler monkeys scream loudly. (c) A fierce-looking mandrill. (d) An indri leaps 30 feet (10 m). (e) A slow loris. (f) The aye-aye listens for insects hidden under bark. (g) Primates try to avoid boa constrictors. (h) These olive baboons live in a grassy clearing. (i) A black spider monkey. (j) For warmth, ring-tailed lemurs huddle together. (k) While a gorilla nurses her new baby, her one-year-old swings in the trees and the male watches for danger. (l) A black gibbon seizes a bird in midair. (m) Before it went to sleep, the orangutan covered itself with branches and leaves. (n) Using a stick, a chimpanzee digs termites out of their nest. Nearby its young play. (o) The smallest primate is the grey mouse lemur, 6 inches (15 cm) long. (p) A golden lion marmoset monkey flees from an eagle.

with one another, they make sounds, hug, kiss, and hold hands. When a chimp is happy, angry, sad, surprised, or afraid, the emotion shows on its face. Chimps feel strongly toward the members of their families. They even make friends with other chimps. When chimps play, they exercise, explore the world, and learn how to get along with one another.

We human beings are also primates. Using our well-developed brains, we have changed the world. Before there were human beings living on the earth, there were other species of animals. We share the earth with all living things. Animals live in our cities, even inside our homes. Every year we discover new animal species. The more we learn about animals, the more we understand life on the earth.

Because people use so much land and work with machines that pollute the air and water, many animals have been killed and entire species are in danger of disappearing. More and more people are now trying to help save these animals. Only we can make the air and water clean again and make sure there is enough space where animals can live. By respecting animals and letting them live, we will always feel welcome in the animal world.

Two human beings learn about the animal world.